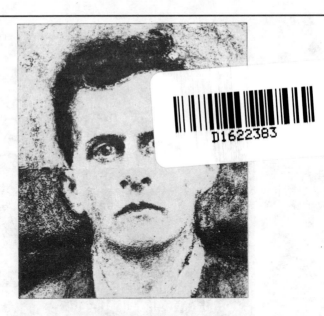

LUDWIG WITTGENSTEIN
The Duty of Genius

RAY MONK

"Ray Monk's book on Wittgenstein is a marvellous work. Monk's narrative is the perfect setting for the riches of quotation from Wittgenstein's letters, notebooks and conversation, which reveal more fully than ever before, the inner nature of that most extraordinary genius." *Prof Sir Peter Strawson*

"A fascinating biography which brings much fresh material to light and clarifies the relationship between Wittgenstein's philosophical work and his emotional and spiritual life." *Dr P M S Hacker*

Jonathan Cape   £20.00   ISBN 0 224 02712 3

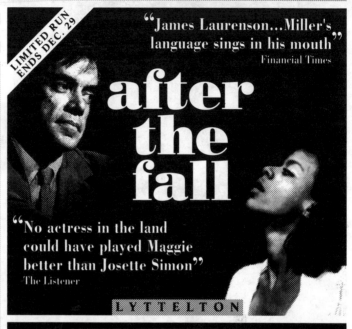
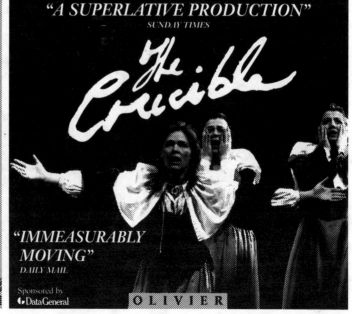

DEATH OF
A HARVARD MAN

34

Penguin

Editor: Bill Buford
Commissioning Editor: Lucretia Stewart
Assistant Editor: Tim Adams
Editorial Assistant: Ursula Doyle

Managing Director: Caroline Michel
Circulation Director: Sarah Bristow
Financial Controller: Michael Helm
Publishing Assistant: Sally Lewis
Subscriptions: Carol Harris
Office Assistant: Stephen Taylor

Picture Editor: Alice Rose George
Picture Research: Sally Lewis
Design: Chris Hyde
Executive Editor: Pete de Bolla
US Associate Publisher: Anne Kinard, Granta, 250 West 57th Street, Suite 1316, New York, NY 10107.

Editorial and Subscription Correspondence: Granta, 2-3 Hanover Yard, Noel Road, Islington, London N1 8BE. Telephone: (071) 704 9776. Fax: (071) 704 0474. Subscriptions: (071) 837 7765
A one-year subscription (four issues) is £19.95 in Britain, £25.95 for the rest of Europe and £31.95 for the rest of the world.
All manuscripts are welcome but must be accompanied by a stamped, self-addressed envelope or they cannot be returned.

Granta is printed by BPCC Hazell Books Ltd, Aylesbury, Bucks.

Granta is published by Granta Publications Ltd and distributed by Penguin Books Ltd, Harmondsworth, Middlesex, England; Viking Penguin, a division of Penguin Books USA Inc, 375 Hudson Street, New York, NY 10014, USA; Penguin Books Australia Ltd, Ringwood, Victoria, Australia; Penguin Books Canada Ltd, 2801 John Street, Markham, Ontario, Canada L3R 1BR; Penguin Books (NZ) Ltd, 182-190 Wairau Road, Auckland 10, New Zealand. This selection copyright © 1990 by Granta Publications Ltd.

Cover by the Senate.

Granta 34, Autumn 1990

ISBN 014-01-3861-7

VÁCLAV HAVEL

Disturbing the Peace

A Conversation with Karel Hvizdala

Edited and with an Introduction by Paul Wilson

15th October 1990
0 571 16200 2   £14.99

CONTENTS

Come and get into our good books.

DILLONS
THE BOOKSTORE

From the latest novels in hardback and paperback to an unrivalled stock of books on any subject you care to name, there's no better place than Dillons Bookstores to come and browse.

Dillons Bookstores nationwide incorporating Hatchards, Claude Gill, Hodges Figgis and Athena Bookshops.

A Pentos Company

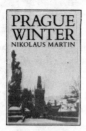

SIMON SCHAMA
DEATH OF A
HARVARD MAN

SPECIAL
NOTICE!

GEO. PARKMAN, M. D.,

A well known, and highly respect-ed citizen of BOSTON, left his House in WALNUT STREET, to meet an engagement of business, on Friday last, November 23d, between 12 and 1 o'clock, P. M., and was seen in the Southerly part of the City, in and near Washington Street, in conversation with some persons, at about 5 o'clock of the afternoon, of the same day.

Any person who can give infor-mation relative to him, that may lead to his discovery, is earnestly requested to communicate the same immediately to the City Marshall, for which he shall be liberally rewarded.

BOSTON, Nov. 25th, 1849.

From the Congress Printing House,(Farwell & Co.) 32 Congress St.

F riday, 23 November 1849.
      The lettuce sat in its brown bag, wilting in the
      unseasonable warmth. By the time that the grocer Paul
Holland had got up the courage to investigate the bag's contents,
the damage had been done. The leaves had gone flabby, pale and
dry. He took the bag from the counter and set it on a cool shelf
at the back of the store in the hope that it might freshen into
resurrection. Such a sorry waste and so unlike Dr Parkman! He
glanced at the wall clock: five o'clock, three hours since he had
marched in, in his brisk, clockwork fashion. The pleasantries had
been, as usual, sparse, and about the weather. Sugar (thirty-two
pounds) and butter (six pounds) had been ordered for delivery to
his house on Walnut Street. The lettuce (bought elsewhere and
dearly, for a salad in November was an extravagance) was set
down on the counter. He would be back 'in a few minutes' he
had said, a few minutes. What Dr Parkman said, he meant, as
many a tenant of his had cause to recall. And regular: my
goodness you could set your watch by him; there never was such
a man for promptness.

      He had left the store, on the corner of Blossom Street, and
walked smartly in the direction of the Harvard Medical College,
the hulking square red-brick building that squatted on North
Grove Street, with its rear against the mud flats of the Charles
River. A number of people had seen him on the way, his angular,
sternly dressed body leaning forward as though his torso were
impatient with his legs for not keeping pace. Two schoolboys
were trading twelve-year-old confidences on the street as the
Doctor flew by. This would have been ten to two, Martha Moore
surmised at the trial, since she had leaned out of her window and
told her young George and his friend Dwight to get themselves to
afternoon school sharpish. They had scurried off across the street
and up Beacon Hill arriving just a minute before the sentence of
'tardy' was recorded in the roll. Just seventy feet away from the
College door, a delivery cart full of pig-iron castings was being
unloaded and weighed by the Fuller brothers in front of their
West Boston Foundry. In the midst of their clattering and
heaving they too remembered seeing the Doctor pass swiftly by
up North Grove Street.

15

Thus he entered the building he liked to call 'a piece of the Holy Land.' Did he emerge again? Some believed it must have been so, for they saw him at different times on that Friday afternoon, cutting a swathe through the Thanksgiving crowds, his stove-pipe hat before, his frock-coat tails flying aft. A clerk in the Registry of Deeds saw him on Causeway Street; a grocer saw him at the top of the West End on Court Street; an ex-tenant saw him in the centre of town near Milk Street in mid-afternoon. As the sunset was drawing on, Mrs Abby Rhoades and her daughter Mary, who had been shopping for wool muslin, passed him on Green Street where he folded himself in two in a deep, polite bow.

Could all these people have been deluded? It was not as if George Parkman was easily swallowed up in a throng. His bustling presence was a fixture on the streets of Boston just because it seemed to proclaim his eccentricity, his determination to announce 'Know ye who I am; of what I am made.' Making a point of neither keeping a horse nor taking a carriage, he walked everywhere, collecting his own rents, inspecting his buildings, even, as the Universalist paper *The Trumpet* noted, doing 'what some proud but poor men refuse to do, carrying bundles in his hands or under his arms to his own house.' He was, in short, the paper concluded triumphantly, a *pedestrian* and wore his pedestrianism like a coat of arms. Rather too many times he told the story (bizarre but true) that his only reprimand at Harvard had been for 'excessive walking on the Sabbath.'

Oliver Wendell Holmes, the Dean of the Medical College, turned these habits into a portrait of the perfect Yankee—exacting yet philanthropic, wealthy yet austere: 'He abstained while others indulged, he walked while others rode, he worked while others slept.' Dr Parkman was a fine vindication of those who believed that a physique and physiognomy announced the man within. He was all bones and sinew, with no cushion of fat on him to suggest much in the way of genteel ease or languor. His face, with its long nose and pointed chin pulled forward by an underbiting jaw, looked as though it had been sharpened into the shape of the crescent moon: a Yankee Mr Punchinello. It was a face that spoke of direction and urgency like the face of a ticking watch.

For time, after all, was the Yankee's capital, placed in his hands by a watchful Providence. It was not something to be frittered away on vanities, but demanded husbanding, investing, spending only where it could bear the rich fruit of interest. And Dr George Parkman, as all who knew him recalled, was one of God's walking chronometers.

Seen sideways on, George Parkman appeared two-dimensional, all points and principles, a lean long-shanked man of means. This was the way in which the chronicler of *Our First Men* classified him. Worth: $500,000; 'bred a physician but practices as a speculator in real estate; owns a vast many cheap built tenements let at high rates and as he is his own rent collector and keeps no horse is seen moving through the city.'

But this crude caricature scarcely did justice to the wonderful strangeness of the Doctor. For the 'speculator in real estate' was also a man of passions and mysteries, medical, literary and zoological. For two days in the bitter February of 1834 he had worked with James Audubon and his son, coats off, desperately attempting to suffocate a golden eagle with charcoal and sulphur fumes so that the ornithologist might sketch it without plumage disfigured by the gun or the knife. But while the thick yellow vapours sent the men choking and rushing for the door, the great bird sat erect on its perch, its eyes glinting, body defiantly and resolutely alive. Despairing of any other solution, father and son Audubon resorted to the usual execution, one tethering its talons and wings while the other stabbed at its heart. What had begun as rational ended in hysteria; what begun as mercy ended in murder.

This was not the end, though. If Audubon was to have his sketch he had to get to work before the rigor mortis set in. So for five days he worked to try to breathe life into his drawing, sweating by the fire or shivering as the embers died. He became sick and crazy with the effort; took to his bed, tortured with guilt at what he had done. Parkman, who was managing the Boston subscription for Audubon's great volumes, felt doubly responsible as partner and Doctor to the 'Woodsman of America', and had his wife nurse him back to health with pots of tea, bowls of chowder and liberal small talk.

Parkman knew all about human frailty and the way in which it grew from some twisted root into a great trunk of disorder and proliferated branches and twigs throughout the body and mind. His family was full of such bolting growths. He himself had been drawn to medicine as a way of dealing with the infirmities he had experienced as a boy. He had not been 'bred' a physician but had made himself into one by hard labour and stubborn determination.

In 1811 Parkman sailed for France in the USS *Constitution*. He reached Paris at the Imperial zenith and found a city that flattered itself on being the new Rome: virile, benevolent and invincible. An arch was being constructed at its western end that would recall, but supersede, that of Trajan. The horses of Saint Mark and the Madonnas of Bellini had been made over as French. Every day saw some new fantasy realized in costumes of velvet and gossamer, sauces of cognac and cream, buildings of marble or spun sugar.

Such refinements were not for George Parkman of Boston. Through the good offices of the American Minister Joel Barlow, Parkman was introduced to the living embodiment of Gallo-American cordiality, the Marquis de Lafayette, although it was at a more improbable table that Parkman finally found his mentors. In the pretty suburb of Auteuil, where Ben Franklin had held court in the reign of Louis XVI, Benjamin Thompson, no patriot, a notorious Loyalist who had begun his career in the same Boston dry goods store as George Parkman's father, lorded over the villa that had once belonged to Antoine Lavoisier, the greatest of the old regime's chemists, a man of humanity and intelligence who had been guillotined as a tax farmer in the Terror. Thompson had metamorphosed into 'Count Rumford' (a pumpernickel pedigree), inventor, landscape gardener and social engineer. In a house filled with the broken optimism of the scientific enlightenment, Parkman stood by as the Count, restless and inventive, buzzed and whirred, concocting the perfectly nutritious soup (at lowest possible cost) for the indigent, the most elegant urban park, the perfectly mechanized water closet, projects of mental and corporeal health put into mutually sustaining balance.

This was more to Parkman's liking than Paris modes. *Chez* Rumford he encountered the luminaries of the Institut: Destutt de Tracy, Cabanis, Cuvier, men whose sagacity and public-spiritedness manifested the Napoleonic commitment to the empire of ideas as well as arms (or at least their utility). One man of sombre appearance and high moral deportment struck him as especially superior. This was Philippe Pinel, doctor to the insane at Bicêtre and La Salpetrière. Not many men whose appointment dated from the height of the Jacobin Terror had survived into the Empire, but Pinel's reputation blotted out this embarrassment of chronology. When learned men thought of Philippe Pinel they imagined the scene that vindicated the marriage of science and humanity: the doctor entering the dank screaming prison of Bicêtre with its smells of terror and piss; the insane manacled to walls along with the most desperate criminals, where, in the presence of the incredulous Jacobin commissioner Georges Couthon (himself a cripple confined to a wheelchair), Pinel proposed striking off the fetters that bound the moaning bundles of skin and bones. His hands working hard on his chair, Couthon wheeled himself from the scene and Pinel passed among the demented like an apostle armed with a holy power, freeing them from their shackles. Some of them hung on his coat and trousers like abject animals, crying with adoration and hatred.

Was this not admirable, Michel Foucault? Parkman, at any rate, supposed so. That Pinel had since devoted his life to the principle of the curability of the insane and of their potential rehabilitation into useful society seemed to Parkman a noble use of days. That Pinel's regime among the men of Bicêtre and the women of La Salpetrière (he noted how disproportionately more women lunatics there seemed to be) was one of managing their conduct by rewards and punishments, Parkman thought wholly appropriate. It was inevitable that a superintendent of such houses should be a stern father and judge of the patients if he were truly to be their friend. Parkman enrolled with Pinel and his anointed deputy Esquirol and walked with them through the long wards, noting that the food was nutritious (and not gastro-

19

neurologically disturbing), that the air was salubrious, that those who broke into spasms of violent raving could be restrained without excessive brutality. Parkman was attentive; he marked things in his notebook: the classifications of the insane—*manie, demence, frenesie*; how some lost souls would refuse all sustenance; how others would find any clothing unsupportable.

Parkman dreamed of establishing such an asylum in Boston. It would differ from Pinel's establishments in one important respect. Borrowing from the Yorkshireman Tuke's belief in the therapy of nature, Parkman would build a house beyond the city, on a hill, surrounded by oaks and beeches. He imagined a place much like a gentleman's villa, with a pedimented door, Ionic columns (or at least pilasters) and sash windows, full of light and fresh air. Outside, patients would busy themselves by raising green vegetables, milking cows or gathering honey from the hospital hives. All of this would be administered as Dr Rush had recommended in a spirit of 'mildness, patience, forbearance and encouragement'—though with a strong enough dose of Pinelian firmness to contain disruption. In time, many such victims, now wandering in unreason, would be made reasonable again; those who had lost their true nature would find it.

Before returning to America to begin this work, George Parkman toured Europe to compare other institutions with what he had seen in Paris. He journeyed to the French provinces, to Bordeaux, Avignon, Marseille and then on to Italy. In Rome he avoided the Apollo Belvedere and other specimens of the ideal torso in favour of stricken bodies lying in the *ospedale* where 'the surgeons, as I have seen them in other parts of Italy, were very shabby-looking gentry. In their treatment of ulcers the unfailing routine is to pull off the last dressing and clap on a fresh one, *voilà tout.*' In Florence he sought out Galileo's telescope rather than Donatello's *David*, and, in the military hospital, he moved among beds full of youths whose brilliant uniforms and Napoleonic delusions had been shredded under fire. In one bed lay a twenty-one year old who, Parkman wrote, 'had lost his reason at the moment he was drawn for the army and has been silent, sad and stupid ever since.'

Then in Pisa he beheld a great marvel: a human skin peeled

away entirely from the body, the subcutaneous blood-vessels stained to reveal their capillary tracks. Parkman followed the process of unpeeling with astonishment. That the human casing could, with a snip here and a tug there, be so perfectly extracted seemed to him a miracle of delicacy and cohesion. Once dislodged intact, its oil was wiped clean and the whole dermis hung up to be air-dried. What remained was a garment of translucent parchment that turned creamy yellow-white, mapped with the tracing of the blood paths beneath. It was an empty person, exquisitely designed. If only the filling could be made to match the packing how truly godlike might be the result!

In 1813 he returned to America via London, where in Bedlam he saw lunatics who had committed murder chained to the floor for the rest of their lives. This would not do. Back in Boston Parkman burned to translate Pinel's principles and practices into a Massachusetts asylum, an institution of humanity and reason. He had no doubt that such a place was needed for he had consulted clergymen, physicians and even postmasters throughout the state to determine the exact numbers of the insane receiving, or needing, seclusion and treatment. As a first step he opened a small house in the city where his working methods could be applied, but his sights were set on something much grander, the first asylum in the state.

As luck would have it, the Massachusetts General Hospital (installed in one of Charles Bulfinch's most elegant classical pavilions) was contemplating the same possibility. Parkman, the physician, and Parkman, the property broker, came together to promote the project. His unconcealed desire to be the superintendent of the new asylum was evident in two of his publications. The first was a tract called *Remarks on Insanity*, in which he defined sickness as 'want of control of our feelings and propensities.' In it he set out the Pinelian categories of delirium, melancholy, hypochondria, dementia and idiocy. Each needed its own care and each (even idiocy) had its own possibilities of cure. The second was a pamphlet called *The Management of Lunatics,* in which Parkman imagined an asylum that would 'seldom be viewed as an object of terror,' and where inmates would be received 'with the courtesy due a stranger.' They would, however, be carefully kept from anything that might intensify their distress. This might include other persons, especially those of the opposite sex. Above all, Pinel had taught Parkman that patients had to be watched. Their diet should include items that stimulated the appetite—sausages, anchovies, oysters, smoked beef, ham and salmon—but should they fall prey to the urge to fast (as many did) they would not be forced to feed but would gradually be enticed into sustenance. Should a similar want of attention fail to empty the bladder at healthy intervals more serious intervention was needed—laxatives and emetics. And since physical conditions as much as moral dispositions were the first necessities for a cure, Parkman imagined a warm bath in which the patient would be enclosed beneath a wooden cover as a stream of cold water was dripped on to his head.

He failed to secure the appointment. It was his money, Parkman thought, not his medicine, that had conspired against him, or rather it was what the Hospital thought he had offered *to do* with his money. He had discovered a mansion in Roxbury, a mile south of Boston, formerly belonging to the British Governor Shirley and ideally placed for an asylum of the semi-rustic kind he envisaged—inmates would be gradually coaxed back to their senses while contemplating river banks. To secure the house he had put up a portion of the $16,000 price. He then offered to raise the balance (from among his wide circle of friends and well-wishers). The hospital committee mistook him to mean he would complete the purchase and indeed endow the building from his own resources.

George Parkman hated misunderstandings of this kind. He responded first with awkwardness, then with vexation, then with embarrassment. He saw himself (not unreasonably) as a man of honour in the business: could not the trustees see, that, if he put up all the money, it might appear that he had bought his way into the position of superintendent? All they did see, however, was bad faith and an uninviting entanglement with an eccentric and mercurial man: not the best person to manage a new and delicate enterprise. Instead, Rufus Wyman, a disciple of the

Yorkshire doctor Tuke much favoured by the powerful Holyoke, was appointed first superintendent of McLean Asylum.

It was hard, being spurned in such a manner. Everything that had distinguished him from being a mere creature of his birth, place and property had now been stripped from him. A money matter had come between him and his vocation. Physicians, after all, were practical men, often indeed men of business who seldom hesitated to offer their reputations in the market-place in return for a handsome understanding. Open a Boston newspaper and one could see the most eminent men, the very President of Amherst College Professor Hitchcock, endorse Ayers Cherry Pectoral, professing himself to be 'satisfied that it is an admirable compound for the relief of laryngial and bronchial difficulties.' Indeed it was not that the trustees of the McLean Asylum had been squeamish about the matter of money but perhaps he had not been acute enough at sounding them on their price.

George Parkman, disappointed, relapsed into his dynastically allotted role of a Man of Property. When his father Samuel had died in 1835 and left a great pompous space vacant in the mansion at Bowdoin Square, George became the manager of the family estates. As if seeking compensation for his never-to-be-forgotten indignity, Parkman then proceeded to buy up large tracts of Boston, from the tenements of the South Cove and the wharf streets of the North End, to the tree-shaded sidewalks and churches of the West End. The Parkmans would not be effaced from the city's future. There would be a Parkman Chair of Divinity at Harvard and a Parkman Chair of Anatomy at the Medical College, the new building of which would be constructed on land sold, not donated, by George Parkman. The new jail in Charles Street would be a Parkman property and the United States Court House would be located in a Parkman house.

Not that he forgot about the unfortunate crazed creatures who had touched his sensibilities in the long wards of the Paris hospitals. He wrote about them in the *Boston Medical and Surgical Journal* which, together with the *Medical Intelligencer*, he published from a small press in a back room of his house. He remained 'an authority' and occasionally was called on to testify in court whether a defendant had committed an act of violence while in a fit of insanity. This was only fitting, since so much of his own writing was concerned with detection as well as rehabilitation. It had been proved, had it not, that moral weaknesses or imperfections could easily lead first to impulsion, then to irrationality and finally to mental havoc. Such dire endings could have banal beginnings: a financial failure; the inability of a woman to secure a spouse (for women, he recalled from La Salpetrière, were especially susceptible). He listed the danger signs: 'impatience, petulance, irresponsibility, rashness, avarice, pride, extravagance, dishonesty, political and professional enthusiasm, gourmandising, venereal diseases, intemperance.' Of special concern was what Dr Pinel had called *monomanie*: the hidden growth of some terrible and malignant impulse behind a mask of absolute normality, swelling irresistibly until the day it would erupt in an act which the host was quite incapable of mastering.

What would such a person look like? A bank clerk? A preacher? A doctor? A professor of Harvard College?

The bitterness receded. Boston came to know two George Parkmans. There was, to be sure, the exacting landlord, the omnipresent walking rent-collector. But there was also the Parkman who offered his own house as a hospice during epidemics of smallpox, cholera and scarlet fever. He was often seen at the McLean Asylum in Somerville involved in some project to ease the lot of its inmates. He supplied a piano for the patients and in the fall of 1849 had an organ made for the hospital chapel. The poetry and pathos of insanity had begun to affect him. Caught between a succouring evangelism and raving despair, he took to writing on William Cowper. He was fond of the steady rhythms of the Olney hymns:

> *The Lord will happiness divine*
> *On contrite hearts bestow*
> *Then tell me, gracious God, is mine*
> *A contrite heart or no?*

Such men as Cowper suffered, he knew, and he was made angry by anyone claiming that the insane were devoid of an ability to feel. He remembered a poor demented man in his care 'who became stupid and apparently indifferent to everything, extremely filthy,' but whose first words after weeks of silence were: 'Did you know anyone *half* so wretched as I?' After all, Parkman thought: 'Do dreaming men or unjustly angry, anxious, distressed, envious, suspicious, prejudiced, impatient, petulant, avaricious, proud, enthusiastic, jealous, irresolute, suffer less because their feelings result from delusion?'

On 23 November, at about two o'clock in the afternoon, he went into the Medical College for his appointment with Professor Webster.

His purposes will ripen fast
Unfolding ev'ry hour
The bud may have a bitter taste
But sweet will be the flow'r.

The following appeared in the *Boston Transcript and Journal* on Saturday 25 November 1849:

SPECIAL NOTICE
GEO. PARKMAN, M.D.,
A well known, and highly respected citizen of BOSTON,
left his House in WALNUT STREET, to meet an
engagement of business, on Friday last, November 23d,
between 12 and 1 o'clock, P.M., and was seen in the
Southerly part of the City, in and near Washington
Street, in conversation with some persons, at about 5
o'clock of the afternoon, of the same day.

Any person who can give information relative to him,
that may lead to his discovery, is earnestly requested to
communicate the same immediately to the City
Marshall, for which he shall be liberally rewarded.
BOSTON, *NOV. 25TH* 1849.

2

Friday, 30 November 1849. 'Well, Ephraim,' said Marshal Tukey to the janitor, 'was it the turkey Mr Webster gave you that made you so suspicious?'

'I should say not, sir,' Littlefield replied. 'It were well before that, on Sunday, that I thought I should watch the Professor, and I told the wife I'd do it, even though she was none too happy about such a snooping and a prying.'

'But the turkey, Ephraim,' the Marshal insisted with a determined merriment not appropriate to the moment, 'did you eat it, then, you and Mrs Littlefield?'

'Wouldn't it have been a sin to waste it, with us making the holiday on the pretty little the college pays us.'

'And was it a good bird, the Professor's turkey?'

'Good enough.' The janitor had always been uneasy in the presence of the Marshal. He had a way of looking so hard and direct at you out of those grey eyes that you didn't know what he was up to.

'So on Thanksgiving you had your dinner and then set to work to find the body?'

'I were mighty tired of all the talk, wherever I went, in the market and the Lodge as to how if they were to find the Doctor it would be in the Medical College, and all those queer looks coming my way as if I had something to do with the business. I reckoned seeing as how your men had been through the place, all that was left was the privy vault, and if nothing was there, that would be the end of it.'

'But you thought there might be something there, didn't you Ephraim?'

'I don't know what I thought, sir. I wanted to be done with it, I know that.'

'And the reward, Mr Littlefield,' Marshal Tukey asked, shifting to a less familiar form of address, 'assuming that what we have are the remains of the Doctor; will you be collecting the reward posted by the Doctor's brother-in-law, Mr Shaw?'

'Have I ever said I would, Mr Tukey?' the janitor replied

with a note of anger. A long moment of silence followed. Why, with all that had happened, was he the one to get such questions as these? Why should it be he who had to explain himself?

Littlefield looked round at the other men, three of them sitting on his best green chairs in his little parlour. Mr Shaw's old face looked white and stricken by what he had seen. The younger Dr Bigelow, the surgeon, had his chin cupped in his hands and was looking desolate. He had been rough enough with Littlefield when he had run into his house with the dirt and gashes of his work still on him; had shaken Littlefield, called him crazy and such names. He was quiet enough now, wasn't he? The two other policemen were more themselves. Derastus Clapp, the detective, had his little leather book out and was scribbling something while Constable Trenholm was standing by the door as though expecting intruders.

The Marshal got up quite abruptly as though he were addressing a public meeting: 'Well, gentlemen, I suppose we know what must be done. Secure an order for the Professor's arrest, Mr Clapp; find him and bring him here. He shall see this and we shall see how he conducts himself.'

Everyone but the janitor and Constable Trenholm departed, the detective to Cambridge to seek the Professor; Shaw and Bigelow to their houses on Summer and Chauncy Street. The Marshal walked slowly back to his office, trying to clear his head in the sharp night air.

In the parlour, Ephraim Littlefield sat nursing an unformed sense of grievance.

They made their mark, all those niggling questions from the Marshal. You would think, wouldn't you, after all I'd done, that the Marshal might be more accommodating? Hadn't I saved them from foolishness; hadn't I known what was coming, all along? You learn a lot, tending their stoves, washing their sinks, clearing their trash and generally cleaning up after the professors; not just what they did but what they were. They all thought themselves such gentlemen and some were but some weren't. Mr Holmes now and Mr Jackson, they were the salt of the earth and could say good morning without making it sound like an order, and old Dr Bigelow, who could say a word against him, unlike that son of his with his stuck-up airs and his French cabriolet.

As for Webster, there had always been bad feeling between us, ever since I started as janitor seven years before. Then in '46 when the new College had been built on Doctor Parkman's land, I found myself sharing the lower floor with Dr Webster's laboratory; we got on no better, a good deal worse really. He had always been at me like some yapping dog. Littlefield did you leave the windows open again? Littlefield have you been playing cards in my room again? Well, he never found me at it did he and what if I had, what harm was there in that, a few fellows for company and no damage done to person or property? I knew that Webster wanted to be rid of me, years ago, and how he had told stories to the Dean, but nothing could come of it, could it? And now who was the villain?

Well, I have done some bad things in my time, like many men, but nothing so bad as this. I never liked it, having to sell cadavers to the students for dissection at twenty-five dollars a body, but how was I and Caroline and the children to live on the pittance the College paid me otherwise? In the taverns they called me a Resurrection Man and said that I had dug fresh graves on the Common and on Copps Hill to supply the students, but it was all stories, mostly; only I didn't ask questions of those who gave me the bodies. These days, with all them dying of the cholera and in a filthy state, there was a premium on a clean fresh corpse so I was doing everyone a good service wasn't I, being the middleman? The one time I had gone out in the night to do it myself I gagged from the badness of it and the smell of mushrooms from the earth, and threw up into the grave and swore off ever doing it again.

Now 'Doctor Parkman, in his queer way, he would understand what a man had to do for his living. Didn't he do some rum things himself for the extra penny? And he knew the value of the dollar by God. So when he started showing up at Webster's lectures, standing at the back of the wall, waiting for him to finish, it had to be some business with money. Then ten days or so ago, the two of them had a pretty sharp exchange, Doctor Parkman just sailing into the Professor's back room while he was reading his chemistry book by the light of a candle. The intrusion itself got him steamed up but it got worse when the Doctor fairly shouted at him, 'Are you ready for me tonight?' or some such. Then there was a fair to-do right under my nose, the Doctor with his high voice talking about some mortgage on goods already spoken for and getting red in the face and waving papers at the Professor and him going white and trying to keep calm and myself trying to keep out of it but hear it all at the same time. 'Doctor something must be accomplished tomorrow,' Parkman said to Webster before he left in that hurried way of his, but I never saw him come back.

Then a day or so afterwards, Professor Webster had asked all those questions about the dissecting room vault: the hole where the trash from the cadavers was slung. There had been men down there fixing a leak in the wall next to the coal pen so that the smell didn't get over the building, and now it was covered with earth and dirt to seal it up. Why should he be so interested in that vault and the way down to it, and whether a lantern could be kept lit down there? I told him that I had had trouble doing that when I went to fetch an African skull Mr Ainsworth wanted to macerate and then there was a silence till the Professor said as how he needed some gas for one of his chemistry experiments, and the vapours in the vault would be just the thing.

I hadn't put anything much together then, not seen any connections you could say was peculiar, even after I heard the news of Dr Parkman's disappearance. On the Sunday, when the handbills were plastered up, I had gone out with a whole gang of people to search round some of the neighbourhood and look into some of the Doctor's tenements to see if some foul play had been done to him. That afternoon, about four or so Webster had come up to me by the College and asked me if I had seen him on the Friday and I said, Yes, just before dinner time that afternoon, coming towards the College door. It was then that the Professor struck his cane, a heavy polished thing with some sort of silver knob on it, hard on the sidewalk, so hard he might have cracked it. It was so sudden and so violent that I started a bit and then the Professor went on to tell me as how it was at that very time that he had seen the Doctor in his room and had paid him $483 and some cents owing to him. The Doctor, he said, took it, struck a line through the mortgage paper and dashed off saying he would have it discharged at the Cambridge office.

I wondered at all this information, not having asked it and out it comes just the same and in such detail too, the exact number of dollars and even of cents as if he were a book-keeper. And all the time the Professor said this, he kept his head down not at all like he usually did. Usually he'd look at me direct, through those specs of his, as though he meant something harder, in between the words. But it was the crack of that cane of his that I heard over and again that night; how he didn't hit it true; how the force of it was too much and sideways against the flagstone. Then everything seemed to fall into place: how I'd seen Professor Webster coming down the stairs with a candle Friday afternoon five o'clock or thereabouts much later than ever he did and how when I'd gone in to sweep up his rooms on Saturday like I always did I found the doors bolted from the inside.

I woke Caroline and told her right out I thought he'd done something to the Doctor and how I was going to keep a look-out on everything he did.

'Oh, Eph,' says she, 'I'm afraid you don't know what you're doing and suppose it ain't so and even suppose it is so, do you think the professors would believe one of their kind could do such a thing?'

'I don't know what they'll believe,' I said, 'but all I know is I saw the Doctor on his way here and how he said hard words to Webster about finishing things and that since then things have happened here that haven't happened before and I mean to find out why.'

I had to do most of it myself, since the police were so dull about it. Why on the Monday when the officer Mr Starkweather came with Doctor Parkman's agent to look round the College, they seemed to tiptoe around as though it were a waste of time. And this when Dr Webster's rooms were still bolted fast. When he opened up to my knocking, I showed them how the rooms were arranged, the little laboratory and the private study at the back of his lecture room, with a stair leading from that room down to the lower laboratory. They went down and looked about the dissecting room and the lab but they didn't take much time about it.

Even on Tuesday when Mr Clapp came with two other officers, I wasn't sure they meant business. They gave us some story about wanting to search all the houses in the neighbourhood and getting entry better if they could say they had looked over the College first. Perhaps it changed when the Professor wouldn't come to his door; only after I had banged on it with knuckles and then with fists and then given it a fine pounding as hard as I could. Standing there in that queer cap of his and the blue overalls, he seemed a lot more jittery than the day before, and warned Mr Clapp to look out for what he called his dangerous things in his back room: powders and glass vessels and minerals and such. It's true some of the lads had done some mischief to precious minerals some time back and he got fair worked up then but he seemed more excited about it all than his science allowed for.

It was even more fishy when we went downstairs. Mr Clapp asked about the privy and right away Dr Webster went to unbolt a door to one of the store rooms to turn their attention away from it.

The vault was staring them all in the face of course. Later on they told me that it was too obvious a place to make it likely anything would be put there, and at the time, since I had the lock and key of it and had seen nothing, I didn't give it much thought myself. Still we peered inside it and saw nothing and even went down the little trap door right under the building into the little crawl space. I told them how the only way into the privy and the vault would be to knock a hole in from the underside and none of them volunteered, so we left it at that.

It was that same afternoon that the Professor's manner altered, became slacker, for he unbolted some of the doors at last. When I saw him in his back room the Professor asked me if we had our turkey yet and when I said I thought we might eat out this year on Thanksgiving the Professor went right ahead anyway and made me the gift of one from Mr Foster's next to the Howard Athenaeum. He said he might want an odd job or two done in return, but it still didn't make it less peculiar, him never having given me so much as ten cents before.

Next morning I could hear the Professor moving about downstairs and felt so vexed at not seeing what he was up to that I tried peering through the keyhole of the store-room door, then chipping a piece out big enough to see with my knife. I think I must have made a cracking noise for the Professor suddenly stopped walking about. I laid myself full-stretch on the floor and got a squinny beneath the door, enough to see the Professor coming and going with the coal hod and bundles of wood. The wife came out and saw me and got flustered and told me to come away then and there since we had to do our marketing.

All that morning, though, my mind was far away from sweet potatoes and harvest corn. I was of a mind to do more and see more, but I was still taken by surprise, when I got back, to feel the wall near the laboratory was hot. I supposed it could only be the little furnace that was never used and determined somehow to see if it was truly alight. With all the doors still locked and bolted the only way was to climb up my cellar wall and through one of the Professor's laboratory windows. Just fancy what with him always telling me to shut the windows he had left one unfastened himself. Once in, I couldn't see much fire but a big part of the barrels kindling had gone along with a good part of the water in one of the hogsheads.

So I knew what had to be done, didn't I? It were a shame that it was the holiday to do it, but I reckoned at least the Professor would be at home and I could get on with it undisturbed. We had our dinner on his turkey, the children pitching in with a will. Then in the afternoon I dropped down through the trap with a lantern, a hatchet and a mortise-chisel. It was hard to keep the lantern alight down there and the space was about four feet so I was bent double, my knees on the slimy dirt. In an hour and a half all I could do was to batter through a couple of layers of the brick beneath the privy, all the while choking on the dust and scraping my wrists and knuckles against the stone. At times I thought it were hopeless; that I was a crazy person doing a reckless thing; and at times I was scared that there would be nothing and I should be found out and Webster would have his wish and get me dismissed the way he had long wanted; and at times I imagined some formless thing, a rank jelly might wash in from the Charles and cover me.

I wasn't going on at night, for sure, and climbed out of it in time to take Caroline to the Sons of Temperance Ball as I had promised. There we buttoned our lips and forgot for a while what a state we were in. I danced eighteen of the numbers on the card, not all with the wife. I like my dances and think I cut a good enough figure a strutting and a twirling.

That was but yesterday, but it seems an age. We didn't get back till four in the morning but it was no time to be slumbering so I was up at nine when Professor Webster actually came in to see us in the kitchen. He took the paper from the table and asked if there were any more news of Dr Parkman. He told us that in the apothecary's they had a tale of a woman who had seen a big bundle put in a cab and when they had found the cab (from its number) it was discovered to be bloody inside. 'There are so many flying reports about I am sure I don't know what to believe,' he said.

I wanted to carry on with the work but couldn't take the loneliness of it any more so I went to Dr Henry Bigelow and then to Dr Jackson and told them what I was up to. It was a hard thing since I didn't know if they mightn't bawl me out or forbid me going on with it. But they both said I should persevere, Dr Jackson saying, 'Mr Littlefield I feel dreadfully about this; and do you go through that wall before you sleep tonight.'

I knew I needed stronger tools and borrowed a crowbar from Fullers around the corner, telling Leonard some story about setting a pipe in through a brick wall. 'I guess you do,' he came back, looking at me in a funny kind of way. When I got back to the College I dropped the deadbolt on the front door so as to forestall Professor Webster and told the wife to give four raps if he were to approach. Poor thing she had no stomach to be a lookout but had given up trying to warn me off of it especially now she knew two of the professors had given their blessing to the enterprise.

I wasn't long down there before I knew I'd need something still stronger than the crowbar if I was to get through, what with my hands all bloody and blistered already. I got some gloves and a hammer and a big chisel from the Fullers and banged away till all of a sudden I heard Caroline's three knocks and got up out of the space as quick as possible. But it was only Mr Kingsley and Mr Starkweather and Caroline half-smiling, half-upset at her mistake. I couldn't somehow say anything to them what I was at. A few minutes later, I saw Mr Trenholm, and though he were police too, since I knew him better around the neighbourhood beat I told him and said I might be through the wall in half an hour or so. Then the wife came in and said, 'You've just saved your bacon as Professor Webster has passed in.' He came up to Mr Trenholm and I and mentioned the Irishman who'd paid for a one cent toll with a twenty dollar bill and how suspicious the Marshal thought that was.

Twenty minutes or so later when I was sure that Professor Webster had gone for the day I went back down. It was getting dark, not that it made any difference down in that rat-hole, but I felt the cold even as I was sweating through the labour. I knew there couldn't be much left, yet as the sound of the crowbar knocking against the brick suddenly changed I became afraid again and stopped what I was doing, swiped the dirt away from my eyes and just sat on my haunches for a moment to catch my breath. Then I thought of how far I had come and what was the issue of all this and how there could be no going back whatever the resolution. So I raised myself up against the face of the wall, with my back bent, and gave the mightiest swing with the blunt end of the crowbar and I near as fell forward as I was through. The rush of air from the hole near put out my light and I had to shelter it carefully as I broadened the gap enough to put both the lantern and my face through the opening.

I wanted to scream and cry and laugh all at once. For there they were sure enough, lying in a pile propped up against a mound of dirt. I knew enough about bodies and bones—hadn't I been carting them about all my life?—to recognize what I saw: a pelvis with the doings all hanging down from it, some pieces of leg and the Cochituate water from the sink above running down over them it like some fountain. And until that very moment, even with all my suspicions growing and building up and up, I still had no idea what I might see and had never pictured how it might look. Perhaps I was expecting a body, perhaps nothing, but not these bits of butcher's trash sitting on the wet dirt. They were so white you see, so clean and white.

I scrambled back up as fast as I could meaning to tell Dr Bigelow right away. But when I saw the wife and she saw me, and said, 'Why, Eph dear, what's the matter, have you found something?' I couldn't help but busting out crying and bawling as if I were a babe in terror. She sat me down and poured me a drop of brandy and I got my composure back some, enough to take myself round to Dr Jacob Bigelow's in Summer Street. It was only that he wasn't there that made me go to young Dr Henry Bigelow's in Chauncy Street and tell him my story and Dr Bigelow started a yelling and telling me I was crazy and I regretted ever having come at all. Still we went on to Mr Shaw's where we found the Marshal.

He told me to go back to the College and when I got there I found Constable Trenholm had already been down and seen the pieces of body. Soon after the Marshal and Colonel Clapp and Dr Bigelow and Mr Shaw came and we all went down together in the dirt and dust. I wondered at Mr Shaw wanting to do this, he being more elderly, and as we crawled the sixty feet I thought Mr Shaw might swoon but he stayed strong enough to reach the hole. The Marshal put his head in and asked Dr Bigelow to say if these were human remains or no and he didn't hesitate. He knew this was not the right place for anything that might have come from the dissecting room and told the Marshal so. Just then we heard some running and all started at once, the Marshal pulling out his gun and us all saying at once, 'It's him, it's him,' though when we all got out they found it was only the wife and children running around.

'Mr Littlefield,' says the Marshal, 'this furnace you spoke of. I think we had better take a look at it.'

So we walked into the lower laboratory and Mr Clapp went straight to the furnace, opened the hatch, reached in, as far as he could into the ashes, started a little and pulled out a big piece of bone, grey and sooty. I knew straight away what it was. Mr Clapp stood there for a minute, his own arm holding on to the forearm of another. I went to take a look myself but the Marshal took it from me, as if it were a weapon and spoke with uncommon gentleness.

'Come Mr Littlefield; this is enough. We had better wait.'

And we went back to the parlour and he spoke to me in quite a different tone of turkeys and rewards and such like before he went off leaving me with Constable Trenholm.

It's getting late now and I'm worn out from all this labour. How will it be when they bring him here to see this; how will he regard me who have been his menial all these years?

It must have been eleven o'clock. Caroline and the children were asleep when the front door bell rang. On the steps there was a big crowd, policemen and others I don't know how many. In their midst was Colonel Clapp holding up Professor Webster for he looked half-dead and half-crazed. He looked at me once with fear and rage all mixed up in his blinking eyes. But then he got taken upstairs to his rooms and paid me no more attention.

3

Skyrocket Jack? Oh, he was affability itself, was Professor John Webster, a man who lived to make others cheerful. You could see it in his frame and deportment, an endomorph: plump and padded, curly-haired, a beaming countenance, expansive salutations, a warm handshake, an open door, a thoughtful host, a dab hand at whist (careful to lose to the ladies), a man with a firm grip on the neck of the decanter and a constantly inviting expression. In the cause of conviviality he was resourceful, too. Was he not the inventor of the Class Day Spread—a feast of pasties and dainties and summer punch set out on crisp linen in Harvard Yard? Had he not insisted on fireworks to mark the inauguration of handsome President Everett? His was the other face of Yankeedom—as genial and open as George Parkman's was austere and closed. Only three years separated them (in their Harvard classes, more important than their birth), but, while Dr

Parkman was often taken to be older than his days, John Webster was thought of, by many, as always youthful. Only one voice, and that, later too, dissented. 'His phrenology always struck me unfavorably,' wrote Horace Mann. 'I think his head was terribly wide at the base.'

No one, however, doubted John Webster's devotion to his family. Gathered in the domestic nest were three daughters, invariably referred to in the sympathetic press as 'his three lovely daughters', which was no more than fair comment, there being a fourth lovely daughter married in the Azores. But three were certainly enough to perform perfectly delightful musical evenings of piano, flute and voice for the many guests who came to Cambridge. There were many such occasions, for the Websters were well-connected by family and profession. The Professor's mother was a Leverett, another of the great Harvard dynasties; his wife's sister married into the Prescotts among whom young William, the historian, was losing his sight while pursuing Cortes and Pizarro along the tracks of their conquests. The Robert Gould Shaws were close enough friends for them to discuss spiritualism without embarrassment; the Rev. Francis Parkman Sr was his Unitarian pastor.

In short, not the kind of man one would instinctively place among the criminal classes. A parade of witnesses would file in and out of the box to testify that he was a 'human and peaceable man'. President Sparks, who was bold enough to say that 'Harvard professors do not often commit murder,' had always thought him 'kind and amiable'. Other gentlemen of his acquaintance, prudently considering the consequences of their testimony, would avow his *reputation* to be that of a lamb, while leaving open the possibility that something else might lie beneath the fleece. He was, however, thought to be inclined to 'a quick and irritable temper' by the inventor and Rumford Professor Daniel Treadwell, by the historian Francis Bowen and by Nathaniel Bowditch. He had been upset, even petulant, when ordered to stop decorating Harvard Hall, said the painter John Fulton. But if quick to anger, all were agreed, he would just as quickly forget the cause of offence. His rocket might flare and fizz and whistle but would be harmlessly spent.

No, he could not possibly have done such a thing, thought one of his pupils, James Oliver, for the Professor had been such a milquetoast. 'When I was in College,' he wrote to his defence attorney,

> it was the regular practice to throw things about Doctor Webster's lecture room; drop his minerals on the floor till we fairly pitied him for his meekness. I think I have seen no other Professor bear so much from his students. Indeed it was a common story that his classes had sometimes made him break up the exercise before the house and in tears.
>
> And yet he always told us that he never 'reported' a student to the Faculty because he wished to get along pleasantly with us! Not every professor can say as much after twenty years connection with the College.
>
> I tell you this to show that we did not merely think Dr Webster a 'peaceable man' but we actually despised his want of spirit and continually imposed on him with impunity.

A sorry spectacle, the Professor put upon by his students; even sorrier since his ability to set seed cake and Madeira on the table depended on their presence. It was all very fine for the magnates of the faculty, the Quincys and the Everetts, well-to-do in their own right and made richer by their marriages, to coast along on their stipend. But the Professor's pittance—a paltry 1,200 dollars—could hardly keep the family, much less their social circle, decently entertained. Extra emoluments might be gained from the College if he were to sell a great many tickets to his chemistry lectures. And the opening of the new building in 1846, on Doctor Parkman's land, with its grander spaces, laboratories and dissecting rooms, encouraged him to imagine a new world of instruction: benches crammed with eager, diligent, *respectful*, ticket-paying students.

To his dismay these throngs failed to materialize. Perhaps he was partly to blame. He could never manage the witty sallies, the elegance of Oliver Wendell Holmes upstairs, from whose rooms there echoed hearty laughter followed by studious silence. At least there were some students and he could overlook their loutish misconduct if their tickets were paid. But somehow there were never enough to make good his many obligations, let alone the finer conveniences of life. Such a bitter disappointment, for a man who was now in his prime, who had served the College so faithfully and had such responsibilities—so many unmarried daughters. Grievances chewed at him. Why was the world so unjust? Why had others prospered with so little effort (and so few virtues), whereas he had been singled out for struggle and misfortune?

His adversities seemed all the more cruel when he considered how fair had been his prospects. His pedigree was impeccably Puritan; his grandfather just as much the merchant-prince as old Sam Parkman. He had been born on Anne Street in 1793, before the whores made it their favourite place of commerce, opposite his father's apothecary shop. Removed to Amesbury, the family fortunes had grown, but his father had grown tyrannical, keeping him on a niggardly allowance all through his school and college years. Like George Parkman he had studied with the sainted John Warren at the old Medical College on Mason Street and like him he had travelled abroad in search of more instruction. London, rather than Paris, became Webster's academy; and instead of the howling corridors of Pinel's asylum, John Webster dwelled among the dark oak walls and red tiles of Guys Hospital. In England he developed the taste for poetry which he passed on to his daughters in their evening reading of Milton and Gray. His name appears on the Guys' Register directly below that of a fellow-student, John Keats.

He was not, however, completely free of boyish naughtiness. At Harvard the adolescent Webster earned reprimands from the severe gentlemen responsible for keeping discipline over their adolescent charges. In London, so his uncharitable wife's sister Amelia later recollected, there had been talk of a rape; of flight from the country; of another broken betrothal, another running-away.

Whatever the proximate reasons, in the year that Napoleon

was sent to St Helena, John Webster found himself marooned on the tiny island of São Miguel (St Michael as the Anglo-Americans renamed it) in the Azores. Yankees came to the islands for two reasons: whaling and convalescence. Sixty ships from New Bedford and Nantucket put in each year, and the little inns of Ponte Delgado were full of red-faced men drinking their fill before the hunt. But the blue skies, the merry breezes and a little sulphur spring that oozed and hissed from a volcanic hillside also made it a station for those seeking therapy for rheumatic joints or wheezing asthmatic lungs. John Webster ministered to both sorts: the swaggering salts and the whey-faced invalids.

Beyond the orange and lemon groves, on a hill dotted with alien plantings of cedar and poplar, Mr Hickling, the American consul, lived with his four daughters. Starved for conversation that turned neither on the current price of spermaceti or the curative properties of mud, the family made much of the young physician, and before long John Webster, the affable, expansive, educated John Webster, had turned the head of Harriet Hickling. If medicine was his profession, geology was his passion. On walks along the cliffs, or down in extinct craters from whose floor sprouted giant ferns and spongy beds of moss, the bespectacled suitor did his wooing with impressive talk of epochs Jurassic and Cretaceous. He related the primordial heavings and shiftings, eruptions and settlements, oozes and deposits that had produced, at length, Azores rocks. Meaningful pebbles clicked in his palms as he gently lectured his student. Half listening, Harriet saw a life of grace and dignity, a life at the core of American culture, opening before her: handsome, modern broughams, nutwood-panelled parlours and the agreeable music of informed conversation. She would be off-island at last, rescued from social shipwreck, given the setting her own qualities surely called for.

In Boston, the reality fell sharply short of the dream. Webster went into practice with a Doctor Gorham but was never quite able to live in the style a gentleman-professional required. As junior partner he seemed to be paying more than he earned for equipment and books and the social exercises needed to establish a clientele. When the apothecary father died, further rude shocks awaited him. The fortune, rumoured to be 50,000 dollars, was a small fraction of that, much of the capital being swallowed up in imprudent ventures, or vanishing at the indeterminate golden horizon of Western speculation; much of the rest subsided with the stock of the Charles River Bridge Company.

As George Parkman withdrew from science to business, John Webster went in the reverse direction. Harvard made him a lecturer in chemistry at the medical school for 800 dollars a year, but what the position wanted in remuneration, Webster felt, it compensated for in distinction, or at least potential distinction. To be, one day, a Harvard Professor, to dwell amid men of intellect, erudition and lightly worn religion; to be received, *ex officio*, as a man of culture—this was surely worth the regrettably thin purse that went with all these blessings. But as time went on and he did indeed become one of the Elect, the Erving Professor of Chemistry, and the 800 swelled into all of 1,200, his discontents mounted along with his debts.

How could they have been avoided? he asked himself. He could not ask Harriet and the girls to live in a mean hovel. So the depleted legacy was spent on a custom-built house on Concord Street, with a grandiose portico, a fine library and capacious wine cellars. When it burned to the ground in 1866, long after its owner had gone from the scene, it was known to locals as 'Webster's Folly'. Servants had to be kept. A Professor must needs entertain. He paid for equipping the Medical College, made more expensive since his predecessor in the chair had obliged him to buy his obsolete and ill-used experimental equipment, down to the last cloudy alembic. He needed, in addition, to satisfy the urges for learning that came upon him now and again and prided himself on building indisputably the best geological cabinet in all of Boston. Then there was the mastodon. A gentleman in New Jersey had let him know that a complete skeleton could be his for a mere 3,000 dollars! A whole, undivided mastodon! His dreams were haunted by great curving tusks and a noble, prehistoric cranium. How could he refuse? Perhaps the Dean, Dr Warren, and the College might provide the funds, or at least the major part, and the beast would then be housed in the college museum, its triumphant specimen. But by the time Dr Warren demurred—and the college's part was a dwarfish portion—Webster was already irreversibly committed. Somehow he provided what was called for, and it returned to sit crushingly athwart his shoulders, a mammoth debt.

For ten years John Webster scraped along in such a way, drifting dangerously far from the Bostonian shores of prudent housekeeping; dressing and schooling and dancing his wife and daughters as Cambridge ladies expected to be dressed and schooled and danced. Publications helped supplement the stipend and the sparse lecture tickets. *Webster's Chemistry* became a text-book in American colleges; his translation of the great Justus von Liebig's *Organic Chemistry* joined it on the shelf along with a definitive mineralogicial and geological survey of the Azores.

But it seemed that rocks of the mid-Atlantic would not be enough to spare the Professor painful embarrassment. In 1835, after another speculative disappointment, the Concord Street house had to be sold. Bearing the social disgrace and personal discomfort with commendable fortitude, the Websters removed themselves to Jonas Wyeth's pretty frame house on Garden Street, close to Washington's Elm, where the commander had mustered his men on Cambridge Common. It was certainly not grand but would do, especially on a long-term lease with option to buy. If there was no portico, there were at least pilasters and an attic for the servant who could survey the street from a sweetly cross-hatched dormer window. There was a garden, not spacious, but land enough for the Professor to transplant hydrangeas and azaleas that had been carefully shipped from St Michael by his sister-in-law.

The retrenchment was not enough. In 1842, creditors became distressingly importunate. But why else should a man have friends if not to turn to them in his (temporary) hour of need? He went to George Parkman, a gentleman famous for his timely loans, and borrowed 400 dollars. Five years later he needed further succour, and a syndicate of Harvard colleagues and friends—Prescotts, Bigelows, Cunninghams—rallied round to come up with another 2,432 dollars, the odd figure incorporating the balance owing to the Doctor. As security for this substantial sum the Professor reluctantly put up his most cherished possession—the collection of geological specimens and minerals. The university had obtusely declined to acquire this from him notwithstanding all the pains he had taken to perfect the cabinet; it should now be used at least to liberate him from exigency; surely his friends would never call in the collateral.

When the next crisis arrived—for they came now at ever-shortening intervals—he looked around for further help. He dimly recalled his father's claims of a distant relationship to the family of the British knight Sir Godfrey Webster who had taken his own life but had left a reputedly vast estate in Maine. Might there be anything in this kinship, he wrote to his friend the historian George Bancroft? Not, of course, that he was imagining anything might be *gained*, any claim on the estate, that is, but was the kinship itself sound? Did Bancroft know anything about the property and its legatees?

With these baronial fantasies evaporating, the Professor had no recourse but to seek help from his friends yet again. He went to see Robert Gould Shaw in Summer Street. A gift was offered. John Webster insisted it should be a loan. As security the Professor reluctantly put up his most cherished possession—the collection of gems and minerals.

'Just a minute,' said George Parkman, when his brother-in-law and partner Shaw casually mentioned this new loan in their office; just a minute, there is an indecent repetition here! This security is no security; it is already mortgaged to me and others foolish enough to indulge that feckless man his vanities. Those things are not his to make over as he pleases again and again.

This affront to right dealing, this naive fraud, this abuse of friendly generosity stirred inside George Parkman a monstrous outrage. When John Webster applied for the Harvard post, Parkman had lent his good services to secure the appointment. Parkman and his family had, from their Christian fellow-feeling, sustained this ridiculous and unworthy man through many years of slovenly and erratic conduct, if only for the sake of the College and his wife and children. Was this how such charity was repaid, the perpetration of a clumsy underhand trick as though his friends and creditors were so many fools to be carelessly palmed off with an airy wave of the hand. He had forfeited the right to friendly consideration. If the man chose to behave like a common Irish rogue, he should be dealt with like one. In the alleys of the North End he had begun and in the North End he should doubtless finish.

So George Parkman turned agency man, pursuing his debtor wherever he could find him, at card parties and concert suppers; at the medical school annual inaugural address directly in front of his colleagues, his disconcertingly white false teeth barking reproaches in corners of the room. As Webster became evasive, so Parkman harried him wherever he could be found. During the first weeks of November he was bold enough to enter the lecture room (it was after all a Parkman property) and stand at the back, waiting for the class to end, with a silent expression of stony determination.

What was Webster to do? Only one way out of his predicament suggested itself. By the third week of the month he should have accumulated enough fees from lecture tickets to allow him to pay off the Doctor, though he had been relying on those sums to settle with the tradesmen who were descending on him with their bills and charges.

Then one afternoon, Seth Pettee, who collected the fees from the students and made them over to Webster's account, called on him, looking sheepish and red in the face. There was 275 dollars remaining from one book of tickets; nearly another 200 from a further batch.

But, well, Pettee stammered, Dr Parkman had been to see him, asking, well, demanding the monies be surrendered directly to him in settlement of the Professor's debt. Of course, rest assured, he had done no such thing and had made the Doctor understand that he was certainly not authorized to pay the money to anyone but Webster. Parkman then uttered something pretty hard, such as 'the devil you have,' and added that it was too bad that this had happened for now Parkman should be obliged to *distress* Dr Webster and, what was worse, his family. By this Seth Pettee imagined Parkman meant some sort of legal proceedings, but he could not pass this on to the Professor, still less what Dr Parkman had asked him to communicate, namely that Parkman thought him neither an upright nor an honourable man.

At the news of this latest indignity, a smarting sense of impotence and humiliation rose inside John Webster. Was it not enough that poor Harriet should be forced to make sharp economies at home? She had even been obliged to go so far as to enter into secret commercial practice, buying brilliantly coloured and woven fabrics from the looms of St Michael and Fayal and re-selling them to dressmakers in Boston. If reports of her little business should ever become public how would she bear the mortification? Though that would be nothing compared to any kind of ordeal in the courts.

A note arrived at the college for the Professor bearing George Parkman's attacking hand. It minced no words, threatening exposure and disgrace, the distraint of the law. A week later the Doctor arrived in person, walking directly into his back room while he was preparing a lecture as though he were some sort of tenant-at-will being threatened with eviction. He did not even have the decency to wait until I was out of the way but proceeded directly to demand in a high, imperious tone, that 'something must be accomplished.'

Very well, something would be accomplished. The visit had been on Monday, the nineteenth. The following Friday, the Professor called at Dr Parkman's house on Walnut Street, early in the morning, to propose a meeting that afternoon. Some form of settlement was intimated. Later the same morning the anxious Mr Petttee called again with a small but welcome cheque. 'I shouldn't worry,' said Webster to reassure his visitor. 'Doctor Parkman is a peculiar sort of man; rather nervous, don't you know, subject to aberrations of mind. But you will have no further trouble with him now for I have settled with him.' Mr Pettee went away much relieved.

A week passed in Boston and Cambridge. Thanksgiving approached and to greet it the weather had turned suddenly sour and cool.

On that Friday evening, while the last remains of autumn warmth hung in the air, Professor Webster walked away from the College and took himself to Brighams where he ate a mutton chop for his supper. He next stopped in at Kidder's pharmacy to buy himself a bottle of Cologne, after which (in the spirit of the new frugality), he took the omnibus back to Cambridge. That evening he and his wife walked the girls to a party at the Batchelders and themselves went on to the Treadwells for a lively game of whist with friends and neighbours. Nothing untoward punctuated the usual, scattered conversations though there was too much dull technical talk of recent advances in mechanical ventilation for Harriet Webster's liking.

That night, her husband confided in her. He had, at last, he said, settled with Dr Parkman, to the tune of 483 dollars and some loose change, paid in person that very afternoon. The Doctor had taken it with his usual directness and without comment had struck a line through the mortgage, promised to go to Cambridge to have it properly discharged and had peremptorily exited at speed. In the circumstances, and after all that passed between them, he implied, he was not inclined to have him delay for the sake of mere social formalities. And there was an end to it.

The following evening the Professor read aloud from Milton's *L'Allegro* and *Il Penseroso* to the family gathered in the parlour, together with the evening's guest, Miss Hodges.

> *Hence, loathed Melancholy,*
> *   Of Cerberus and blackest Midnight born*
> *In Stygian cave forlorn*
> *'Mongst horrid shapes, and shrieks, and sights unholy . . .*

Next morning, a Sunday, earlier rumours that Doctor Parkman had disappeared were confirmed by handbills liberally pasted about Cambridge

Surely, the Professor told his wife, as someone who had seen him on the very day he had gone missing, should he not let the family know?

Not this morning, replied his wife, since his brother will be at church.

After chapel, not in the North End but closer by in Harvard Yard, the Professor took an early Sunday dinner and made his way in the cold rain to Boston. Everywhere he went he announced what had taken place the previous Friday; how Dr Parkman had indeed come to see him; how he had paid him what was due; how he had departed at speed and that that was the last he had seen of him; how he trusted, since Dr Parkman was such a man of his word, that he had indeed cancelled the mortgage. He told this to Parkman's nephew Mr Blake at three o'clock; to Ephraim I a few minutes later, rapping his cane on the ground for emphasis; and he made the same announcement to the Reverend Francis Parkman at his house.

That family, increasingly desperate and anxious, was expecting something more than such a report, delivered as it was, thought Francis, in so very business-like a manner. John Webster was a friend of so many years standing. When his presence had been announced by the servant, the family's troubled gloom had momentarily lifted, for he had always been ready with words of kindness and sympathy. But on this afternoon his behaviour was so peculiarly hasty that it verged on discourtesy.

The days petered out towards the holiday. The Professor was busy with his last classes at the college, but was at home at regular times for dinner and for tea. He played his flute; the girls sang; he tended to the garden where the grapevines needed their autumn trimming. The whole college, on both sides of the Charles River, hummed with stories of the missing person. Yes, he had to tell colleagues, neighbours, he had seen him that Friday; yes, the police had of course searched the college but had found nothing that might help.

More handbills went up around town. The day before Thanksgiving the Professor was stopped with the girls at a toll-house on their way to a party at the Cunninghams and observed a new notice. He read out loud to them:

$1,000 REWARD

Whereas no satisfactory information has been obtained respecting

DR GEORGE PARKMAN

since the afternoon of Friday last and fears are entertained that he has been murdered, the above Reward will be paid for information which leads to the recovery of his body.

Robert G. Shaw

'W ill it be found, Pa?' Catherine asked
'I'm sure I don't know my dear,' Dr Webster replied, 'everything is being done that may be.' At the Cunninghams, some mischievous party asked, 'Do you suppose, Dr Webster, that as the last person to see Dr Parkman you may yourself be under suspicion?'

'Why,' he retorted amiably enough, 'do you imagine I *look* like a murderer?'

Polite laughter rippled round the room.

4

It has never been easy to keep a secret in Boston, especially if the secret concerns mischief. Since the time of the Puritan Governors Bradford and Winthrop, publicity has served as a form of social cleansing. If a wrong has been done, it has also been done to the community. So the whole congregation of the faithful has a right, a duty, to hear of the deed, to mark the wrongdoer, to accept his atonement, to pray for healing and the restoration of grace. No one understood this better than Marshal Tukey, the inspected Inspector who instituted the famous 'shows' of pickpockets and other riff-raff at his offices where good citizens could come and gawk and judge or, if the mood took them, upbraid and accuse. The essential thing was a vigorous humiliation, a modern pillory, something that would not be forgotten by the righteous and the unrighteous alike.

A great Boston murder, though, has generally been a different kind of show—an interruption that pushes aside the quotidian, provokes public utterances on the state of the times, demands sermons, editorials, predictions of doom, messages of redemption. In all these commentaries the malefactor, especially the unlikely malefactor, is represented as the captive agent of the real criminal: money. Professor William Douglas of Tufts University who battered his greedy whore Robyn Benedict to death in 1985 did so from desperation that he could no longer afford her. Charles Stuart, the Newbury Street fur-salesman, killed his pregnant wife in 1989 so that he might build his palace-in-the-air, an up-market restaurant, on the insurance proceeds. In 1850, God's appointed fulminators saw in the act of a professor who would fecklessly destroy his honour, his reputation, his family, his life, all for a paltry few hundred dollars, the unmistakable warning of God to idolatrous Babylon.

On Saturday, 1 December 1849, a statue to the Antonine sophist Aristides was unveiled in Louisburg Square, at the topographical and moral centre of Beacon Hill. His *Heroi Logi* is the peculiar autobiography of a man in whose daily life the spirit of Asclepius, the healer, constantly intervenes, saving the storm-tossed mortal from calamity. At the gracefully understated ceremony, a polite group of gentlemen in stove-pipe hats and bonneted ladies applauded (without removing their gloves) as a sheet dropped to reveal a peculiarly less-than-life-size sculpture of the spiritually directed diarist and orator. On the same morning, a crowd of men, many in mufflers and knitted caps, gathered about the front door of the Harvard Medical College. They were curious and noisy; some were angry. They had caught the trail of rumour as it had snaked its way about the city since dawn, up from the river to the West End and down into Mayor Quincy's market where the vendors of greenstuffs and pumpkins and the drovers of cattle met to exchange gossip over warm beer in the early morning. In no time at all the rumour had travelled on, past the Market down into the Irish North End where the memory of Dr Parkman was transformed from an exacting landlord into a sainted benefactor. Folk remembered acts of kindness: a bottle of crimson linctus brought for a small child with a ragged cough; the surprising appearance of men sent to repair a leaking roof and who, when finished, left no bill.

If the Doctor now seemed transfigured as the Healer, the Medical College where, it was said, pieces of him had been found, was plainly a place of cold death and hot damnation. Everyone knew that bodies had been prised from fresh graves; yes, and the bodies of the poor, even children, from Copps Hill and the Neck to supply the anatomists' tables. Now there were not enough even of the dead so the dark doctors had turned to the living for their inventory. A place for the Devil's work! Down with it; sack it; tear it asunder; let fire consume its poisons!

At eight o'clock in the morning when Marshal Tukey and his officers had to use their sticks to enter the building, there were already fifty irate people. By midday there were 500 and the noise was more ominous; by the late afternoon a crowd of 2,000 jammed outside the gates and down North Grove Street all the way to Cambridge Street. Sticks and fists were being waved about. It was too ugly for his fifty policemen to contain even if every last one of them were taken off their beat and left the rest of the city to villains. So the Marshal went to see Mayor Quincy and the Governor and had their assent to mobilize the militia at Roxbury that night. As darkness fell he periodically lifted his face and sniffed the night air, like a big animal, alert for a whiff of wood-smoke.

He knew, after all, what the public did not yet know, though it could not long remain hidden. He had seen what they had not seen. The Marshal supposed himself a hard enough man and in his time he had looked at things that would make other men swoon away. He had lived too long in the company of vice and cruelty, and knew the devilry it could do. But when he thought of the grisly slop he had seen yesterday night and again today his gorge rose. As he understood the meaning of the word 'sensation', it was something a man felt, not reflected on, something that crawled on his neck or swam in the tank of his belly. This was a sensation; something he could apprehend but not comprehend.

Thank God for Coroner Pratt, not a man to fool around

with niceties, a true professional man after his fashion. The Marshal's own men, he thought, liked it better upstairs, emptying desks, listening to Littlefield collect clues for them, the spots on the stairwell, rags and cloths and the like. But it was downstairs, in that dark, oppressive place that the real business had got done. Once some lamps were lit, Mr Pratt had just reached his arm into the furnace slag and pulled out pieces of bone. A piece of jawbone, with mineral teeth all fused together by the fire and sticking to a blackened lump of wood; a long grey bone he thought a tibia; a finger; a toe; odd teeth. He would bend and rise, bend and rise, his whole arm inside the dead oven as bits of the man were extracted.

Constable Eaton had run off to puke but all of this was nothing to what followed. It was Constable Fuller who found it, the tea-chest. It had been sitting there all week, delivered by the express man Sawin, full of minerals and a couple of bags of tan that the Professor said he was using for an experiment with leather. Fuller had smelled something bad, something deeper and sweeter and fouler than any minerals, and had reached down and when his fingers had grasped something cold and repellent had yelled for his boss like a child in pain. When the box was emptied they were staring at a headless trunk. For a fleeting second the Marshal thought of prints he had seen of antique torsos, their necks and rumps taken off by the casual accidents of time. But this was hackabout trash, a sallow length of flesh and bone with a great mat of hair clinging to the back, an inch thick, grey and curling. Inside the body cavity were a lung, a kidney, the spleen—offal—and shoved into its cage was a whole thigh, held hanging by a cord.

After that it was difficult to pay attention to the details: the bowie knife in the chest with the tan and potash; a second knife found upstairs, this time exotic-looking with a curved blade and a silver hasp; the saw, suspiciously free of stain or spot, that Starkweather brought down from the upstairs laboratory; the relentless Littlefield bringing him stained pieces of towel.

That afternoon and the following morning members of the Coroner's jury—Brewster the printer, Restleray the chemist and the rest, evidently men of strong stomachs—were brought to the

College to look at the remains. There was a medical committee, some of them close acquaintances and ex-students of John Webster. The pathologists, anatomists, chemists and dentists studied what there was to study: bones, teeth, organs, hair, as well as stains, blotches, chemicals. They separated them, classified them, labelled them, reported on them. The jury listened to their presentation in private but not quite as privately as they imagined. For a resourceful team of penny-press reporters had bribed their way into the cellar beneath the ward room and were listening attentively at an air vent when they were caught, one sleuth speeding away, the other dragged before Coroner Pratt who gave him a severe dressing-down.

For better security the Coroner's hearing was removed to the Court House, where on 14 December, two weeks following the discovery of the remains, they were declared to be those of Doctor George Parkman. A further declaration was made stating that the deceased had met his end 'by blow or blows, wound or wounds . . . inflicted upon him by the hands of said Doctor John Webster, by whom he was killed.'

The mortal remains of Doctor George Parkman were given the funeral rites on 6 December. A long train of carriages had followed the hearse on which lay a coffin, lead-lined within, silver-plated without. Reporters had scrambled along the procession not scrupling as to whom they asked or for that matter who answered their questions. Many were shut out from Trinity Church on Summer Street, its rusticated masonry and crenellated tower protecting the coffin from vulgar intruders. The mortal part of Doctor John Webster had meanwhile already rallied from the prostration of arrest, accusation and detention. Though he had to withstand the inevitable chaffing from the many rogues who were in the Leverett Street lock-ups pending trial, he often seemed in better spirits than they. By the Monday following his ordeal, the Professor was already making arrangements for his own housekeeping and sustaining his role as a Boston benefactor by nourishing his fellow inmates (however disrespectful) from his unwanted victuals.

Franklin Dexter, Webster's cousin and attorney, was one of

the first to visit. The signs of trauma—disarrayed clothes, a bad odour of fear and cold sweat—were still written on John Webster, but given the ordeal to which he had been subjected, Dexter thought, any man, including himself, would have looked as bad. Besides, what was alleged was absolutely inconceivable: a monstrous and abominable tissue of circumstantial evidence, of unsupported innuendos and defamatory incriminations. Let him recover himself a little, receive some nourishment and the succour and loyalty of friends and family, and all would surely be explained. 'Those bones are no more Dr Parkman's than they are my own,' Webster told his cousin, and it could hardly be astonishing to discover dismembered cadavers in a medical college.

The family arrived; wife and elder daughters managing to contain their misery and horror for the sake of Papa, who remained, as they insisted, an *angel*; the youngest, Catherine, quavering on the edge of tears. They brought him comforts and dainties; dried flowers and a little fruit cake, dark with spiced rind and molasses. As days passed he seemed altogether changed again into something resembling their pudgily amiable, sentimental father. He asked them about the neighbours, the garden, Harvard gossip, as if he were confined to an infirmary bed and expecting an early recovery and discharge.

Nor had Harvard yet disowned him. A procession of his learned colleagues made its way to the Leverett Street jail: not least President Sparks, Henry Wadsworth Longfellow and Edward Everett who wrote to his friend Sidney Brooks that

> it is beyond all comparison the most painful event in our domestic history. Dr Webster was my classmate, my playmate from a period still earlier. I have known him from our earliest boyhood. His family, a wife and three daughters are most amicable and accomplished persons: universal favorites.

And in the weeks to Christmas, when the Boston newspapers (all fifteen of them), were busy speculating on the degree of the prisoner's guilt, John Sibley, the college librarian reported that 'the professors pooh at the mere supposition that he is guilty.' They knew him too well, his 'artlessness and unfamiliarity with crime of any kind;' more important, 'his uniform tenor of conduct since the disappearance of Dr Parkman has been such that the excitement, the melancholy, the aghastness of everybody are incredible.' Yet he added, dolefully, 'the vicinity of the Medical College, State Street, the newspaper offices are crowded and thronged. People cannot eat; they feel sick.' The College was in a state of siege. Life had become intolerable, the faculty having to run a gauntlet of jeers and curses to get in at the front door; snouty faces pressed against the windows; the occasional projectile flung hard at the window panes. Meeting at Dr Jacob Bigelow's house the beleaguered professors decided to call a recess of three days to allow the inflamed situation to cool. They could then mourn the loss of their benefactor and recover their own composure. What were they to do; what were they to believe? As colleagues, friends, who had known John Webster for more than twenty years, who had tolerated his petulant eccentricities, warmed to his boyish enthusiasms for fossils and ancient skeletons, they could not imagine him to have done such a thing. To suppose that he had would mean setting their human understanding at naught; that they too (for how different were they?) might be capable of such a deed. It would mean searching through George Parkman's publications on the insane for signs of the double-personality that could present a meek and cordial face to the world and, on occasions, assume another countenance of unspeakable ugliness and rage.

And yet, they were men of science. Certain evidence had been presented that they could not deny. Men of serious repute and professional distinction had given their opinion against the Professor. At any rate it was their judgement that had become the verdict of the Coroner's court. The thing to do, Dean Holmes thought, would be to appoint Dr Horsford as a substitute lecturer, so that the students would not suffer, without in any way compromising their colleague's presumption of innocence. If they could not stand against the newspapers' rush to judgement, who then could be relied on to defend the unimpeached integrity of the accused? 'What is a character worth,' wrote Nahum Capen to Horace Mann just before Christmas,

> if by breath of slander or by the floating uncertainty of
> suspicion it may instantly be changed from integrity to
> perfidy, from purity to corruption, from refinement to
> barbarity and from the highest sentiments of honor and
> religion to the lowest capacity of the wolf and the
> bloodhound! What is character—if people are ready
> without fears and doubts to translate the faithful teacher
> to the felon's cell; the good citizen to the lowest depths
> of shameless crime; the friend to the place of the demon
> and to transform the man to the monster.

In Cambridge drawing-rooms it was keenly felt that much of
this guilt by implication—by untested association—was
Boston's doing. Never had the two banks of the Charles
seemed more widely separated. On the north side, humanity,
learning, generosity, prudence, an aristocracy of honour and
morality; on the south side, a shrinking ground of decency
assailed on all sides by creatures from the gutter, the reptiles of
the penny press, the hucksters of rumour and innuendo, the noisy
gaudy *habitués* of the Melodeon, the enthusiasts of the gallows,
Marshal Tukey's world of scoundrels and fast-driving enforcers.

On both sides of the river, though, the deed stained the
snows of the holiday season. Private parties were put off; people
withdrew into their own parlours where they took care not to
mention the names of Parkman and Webster. There was, as one
commentator put it, 'a general check on hilarity.' In the family
circle of the Prescotts, the mood was particularly gloomy since
Mrs Prescott and Mrs Webster were half-sisters. Father and son
Prescott went regularly to see the prisoner and to Cambridge to
offer what comfort they could to the Webster women who,
among other sorrows, were now seriously distressed for their
living and were taking in sewing to make ends meet. Young
William, the historian, was asked by his brother for his understanding
if the entertainment planned to greet his return from Europe was
of a modest and intimate kind, given the sadness and anxiety of
the time.

For John Webster's extended family nothing was more urgent than attending to his defence and procuring him the best possible counsel. There was no shilly-shallying on this account. The greatest attorneys of the Commonwealth, indeed the greatest *men* of the Commonwealth, were directly addressed by his cousin Franklin Dexter to whom all doors on Beacon Hill were habitually open.

Rufus Choate seemed the most promising. His histrionic gifts (in a city where that quality was much admired on stage, in pulpit and print) were unsurpassed. His whole person was a carefully organized dramatic spectacle: the five overcoats removed one-by-one in court; the unattended black hair falling over the dazzlingly ugly face; the astonishing knee jerks and muscular exertions that bewitched the jury; the melodies of the voice and the lethal sharpness of his cross-examinations. The great Choate could do anything. He had, after all, persuaded a jury that a man accused of murdering his wife had done it in his sleep and that a somnambulist could not, by definition, be guilty of malice aforethought.

But the Mighty Choate had his doubts. Anticipating Dexter's offer he had himself spoken to Littlefield, considered the evidence and the Professor's claims and had decided that he must concede that Dr Parkman had indeed met his death in his laboratory. Just how that came about was then for the Prosecution to show and it would, he thought, be no simple matter. Indeed to demonstrate, beyond any reasonable doubt, that the death had been a premeditated act of cold-blooded murder would, he reckoned, be hard, if not impossible. He would ensure that it would be so. But they had to get the matter of the body behind them; for how other than supposing Parkman had gone into Webster's private room, shook himself into several pieces and then distributed them about the building, could one conceivably imagine they got to such places as tea-chests and furnaces and privy vaults?

Franklin Dexter was despondent. Such an admission, he knew, would never be given nor indeed should be sought.

John Webster was less subtle than Choate. He had never swerved from his adamant insistence that the last he had seen of Parkman was his rushed exit from the laboratory holding the money he had been paid; that he had no idea whatever how the remains, if they were indeed his, came to be on the premises. Even now he was beginning to prepare notes explaining everything the Coroner's jury had found so compromising. So much of his defence had to rest on the absolute discrepancy between the vileness of the crime and the normality of his conduct in the week following the disappearance. How could that now be set at naught by such a retraction? No, it was unthinkable, even at the cost of doing without Choate.

No recourse was left but to have counsel appointed by the court. Not that this put John Webster in the hands of unknown or untested persons. Shown a list of attorneys he selected two of the best known and respected: Judge Pliny Merrick, a long-faced, elegant, sober fellow who had left the Court of Common Pleas to become President of the Nashua and Worcester Rail Road and had just now returned to the bar; and Edward Sohier, called Ned by everyone in Boston, who followed Choate in the school of carefully disarrayed dress and slouching manners, the better to spring on the unprepared witness.

When they came to see him twice or more a week, the Professor seemed still to have great difficulty in adding much, indeed anything, to the simple, unequivocal outline of his recollection. But on paper his recall was more elaborate, his speculations bolder. Before the trial in March he would give nearly 200 pages of such details, outlining an entire strategy for the defence to his attorneys.

He sat in his cell, nibbling on cheese, sipping the Madeira brought him by the Longfellows, scribbling this and that as things occurred to him. Protected from the public view by the walls and bars of the Leverett Street jail, some sort of Webster-figure had already been tried, exposed, pelted with excoriation in the press. The author of *The Boston Tragedy* had already decided that 'a black and appalling case of premeditated murder' had been done; that Governor Briggs already knew it to be so and had said as much; that there was the clearest and most instructive contrast between the famously frugal and punctilious victim and his killer, a man of extravagance, negligence 'and total want of economy,' whose pitiful inadequacies to his responsibilities had made him a lunatic and a murderer.

The bill of indictment, handed to the accused (who had not been allowed to appear on his own behalf), put it differently, namely that

> John White Webster with a certain knife which he then and there in his right hand had held, the said George Parkman then and there feloniously willfully and of his malice aforethought did strike beat and kick and upon the head, breast, back and belly, sides and other parts of him, the said George Parkman and then and there feloniously willfully and with malice aforethought cast and throw the said George Parkman down unto and upon the floor with great force and violence there giving unto the said George Parkman then and there as well as by the beating, stabbing, striking and kicking of him several mortal wounds and bruises in and upon the head, breast, belly and other sides of the body . . . of which said mortal strokes, wounds and bruises he the said George Parkman then and there instantly died.

5

Boston Doric: the usual thing. A pompous colonnade, a lofty pediment; a daunting flight of steps, not a temple but a courthouse. Before it, an uncountable number of faces, hats and bonnets, noses red and cheeks raw in the biting March wind, pressed more closely together than propriety or custom sanctioned, bound by a single determination: to get in.

Sixty thousand would see the trial of John White Webster—statistically nearly half the population of Boston—but in reality a mass of the curious and excited, drawn from all over the state, all over the country, and even from abroad. Reporters had been assigned from Berlin, Prussia, and Berlin, Maine; from York and New York. It was the age, after all, of the temerity of professionals; when science and *bildung* were claiming to refashion the nature of modernity. How then could the public miss an occasion to see those claims so outrageously abused?

The Boston police and the magistracy were becoming accustomed to the management of crowds and thought they recognized the delicate boundary that separated a crowd from a mob. What all these people craved, they reasoned, was a taste of novelty and spectacle. In this spirit of turnstile democracy, the police were instructed to ensure a good even flow in the public galleries. Every ten minutes one ticketed crowd would rise amid shuffling and benches and tramping of boots, to be replaced by another as the proceedings continued below uninterrupted if not undisturbed. After a day of this traffic, even counsels and witnesses became accustomed to this mobile human scenery, standing and sitting, exiting and entering, murmuring and shushing.

Everyone in the court room was acutely conscious of being on public view. When John Webster was brought in, he managed gracious smiles and even occasional handshakes for the friends he recognized, the colleagues, kin, all those who had sustained him in his ordeal and who would now, God willing, see their faith vindicated. To some he seemed offensively jaunty. His gait as he walked to the dock, the reporter from the *New York Daily Globe* noted, 'was light and elastic,' suggesting good form in body and spirits (though, the same writer added, for good measure, that the physiognomist would note a countenance suggesting 'strong animal passions, high cheek bones, a mouth with compressed lips, the forehead angular, rather low and partially retreating').

His Honour, the Chief Justice of the Supreme Court of the Commonwealth, was no more immune from the sense of public spectacle; indeed he consciously reinforced it by his alarming mountainous presence. It was not so much that Lemuel Shaw was physically imposing; it was just that his implacable manner made him seem so. Reminiscent of the omnipotent hanging judges of Hanoverian England, he needed no powdered, curled, falling white wigs to assert his authority. He had a thatch of coarse hair; a startlingly ill-favoured countenance; a staring, forward, way; and an unbreachable sense of self-righteousness. He sat like a great warty toad at the centre of the bench, immovable, unblinking, broad nostrils flaring at the suggestion of impropriety, embodying in his bulk the very weight of justice.

Chief Justice Shaw had no doubts about the deterrent efficacy and the moral legitimacy of capital punishment even at a time when it was being called into question. Indeed he was prepared to thrust his certainty on juries, even on prosecuting attorneys who showed themselves hesitant in the discharge of their duty. When the poor imbecile Pierson had been convicted of murdering his wife and two children in Wilmington the previous year, the jury had expressly and unanimously recommended clemency, yet Lemuel Shaw had no hesitation in overruling their squeamishness and sending the murderer to the noose. He had always lived his life in rectitude (even stories that he had been punished at Harvard for throwing snowballs turned out to be groundless) and saw no reason why those who had violated the law ought not to reap the consequences.

So both the Honourable Mr Pliny Merrick (whose physiognomy, as much as his name, suggested some benign Roman consul), long-faced and elaborately courteous, and Mr Edward Sohier (in superbly eccentric mustard vest) knew they had their work cut out in defence. On 18 March, a day before the trial, they went to the jail a last time to ask Dr Webster (no longer Professor for he had resigned his chair following the indictment) if there was perhaps something he had omitted to tell them, something that had either weighed on, or indeed just slipped, his mind? Something, anything of conceivable significance to the case?

No, no, returned John Webster, it is all there in the papers you have from me, enough I should think for you, gentlemen?

The gentlemen looked briefly at one another. Not enough, their exchange of glances said; too much, yes, 200 pages and more of Dr Webster's instructions on how to construct the defence; yet not enough.

It was an extraordinary document, they readily admitted. They could not recall any client in a similar position having so much to say on his account, so many minute details to correct, so many plausible explanations to offer in answering the prosecution. The locking and bolting of his doors during the days after

Parkman's disappearance, for example? Well, many of his colleagues knew that he habitually did so when he had to prepare a lecture or a demonstration. The spots on the floor and stairwell? Nitric acid used in his experiments; nothing more sinister. The business with the big wooden box found on the Saturday? Well, the fact that it had lain outside the lower laboratory all that week quite unconcealed was surely evidence that until *something foreign* had been introduced it was quite innocuous. After all what had it held other than his chemical vessels he used at home in Cambridge, packed up for him and sent into Boston? The bags of tan? They had been sent expressly by a Mr Southwick of Sutton Place so that he could follow, experimentally, a new process of treating leather. One of the skins would in all probability still be found in the wood-house at home. The Turkish Yataghan knife? An item he had brought from home that he commonly used to cut new corks for bottles and models of crystals and the like to display their mineralogical and chemical structure. The potash? Littlefield had procured it, not on Dr Webster's account either.

Yes, with his help, his counsel could cast doubt on the alleged motive, raise further doubts on Dr Parkman's settled state of mind. Hadn't someone at Appleton's, the organ builders, mentioned how oddly the Doctor had looked when he came to see the work being done for the lunatic asylum chapel? And if he certainly had taken to dunning him for the return of the loan, he had actually consented to his re-selling or re-pledging the mineral collection. As for the money used to pay off the debt that Friday, he had saved it little by little at home expressly for that purpose.

To be sure, he could not explain how those body parts ended up on his premises. But was he required to do so? Given the presumption of innocence was it rather not incumbent on the Government to prove that they had come to be there by his particular agency?

Not that he was imputing *anything*, but there was surely another set of connecting circumstances that could be presented with as much credibility as those weighing against him. Who, other than himself, had access through keys to all the chambers leading from his lecture room and down to the lower laboratory and privy? Why, the janitor of course. The Coroner's court and the grand jury had been impressed with the fact that whoever had dismembered the body showed definite expertise in dissection. Dr Webster had not opened a body in twenty years. Littlefield, on the other hand, 'had seen hundreds of bodies cut up, and attended post mortem examinations for years; indeed might be called an *expert*. He knew the ways and difficulties of separating joints, the sternum and so forth, knew how to prevent blood flowing and could no doubt cut up a body more *scientifically* than I.'

The ways in which simple acts of generosity could be turned against him! That turkey, for example. Sawin could testify how he was in the habit of giving birds at the holiday time. And though the janitor denies it, he had given him something each year, last year a dressing-gown used in lectures. Could he be relied on? Counsel ought to whittle away at the man's character; bring out his many acts of negligence; the arguments on that account they had had; his intemperance, not to mention his wife's!

He didn't say that Littlefield had done the deed himself. The key to it all was his long career as a resurrectionist, his notorious recklessness about getting subjects. There was that body of a young girl brought from New Hampshire that suddenly appeared in the College last year. Resurrectionists after all would do anything in these hard times to procure their income. Many cut off heads and sold them separately to specialists in optics. Littlefield would do things that no one else would touch. For 200 dollars he had cleared out all the bodies that had accumulated in the vaults of the old college before it had moved to the new site; something no ordinary sensibility could stomach.

So in all likelihood he had brought the body to the College as a specimen to sell to the students, discovered whom he had acquired and in a funk had cut him apart and tried to burn the remnants. When he found that burning the remnants would take too long he needed to discard the cadaver in some other place. The dissecting room vault was too obvious, but Littlefield knew where the key to the privy was kept; he would have no difficulty in making use of the privy instead. Indeed, now that Dr Webster thought of it, there were many times that the janitor must have used the privy since he so often found the door unlocked when he distinctly remembered locking it.

Was this account any less probable than his doing the deed by daylight in a room when he might have been interrupted by students, or than his attempt to burn the body when the smell would have advertised the deed throughout the building? Surely Counsel could make much of a contrast in character, especially since there had been such an effort to blacken Dr Webster's own in the press, when he had had no opportunity to defend himself? The Attorney-General, already well-known to the family, surely would not stoop to such defamation in an attempt to create a portrait of a murderer? But perhaps Counsel could paint a different portrait. The true likeness? 'It can be fully proved, I think, that I have been a devoted and affectionate father and that my happiness was centred in my home—my habits of instruction, reading with my family are known to many. Witnesses to this I can give a long list of. I am more anxious to save the feelings of my family and friends than almost anything else.'

No wonder Dr Webster had an air of impending exoneration about him as he waited for the proceedings to begin. He had set it out: all the points of incrimination had been explained and were refuted one by one. He did wonder, though, why his Counsel seemed so pensive, so terribly reserved as they prepared for the trial.

6

By habit and by choice Boston takes to its bed early. At the Exchange Coffee House where more than a hundred out-of-town travellers roomed, they signed an agreement on entry to be in by eleven, the decreed 'retiring hour'. But on this Saturday night, with the great event yet unresolved, there were precious few guests back in their rooms, and lamps and candles all over the city were burning late. At the Tremont House, rooms hired for private dinners became blue with cigar fog. Closer to the court-house, the taverns had filled up with gentlemen of the press, sitting out the jury's decision over tankards of ale and taking bets on how long they would be kept waiting. Lads had been hired at fifty cents an hour to stay at the courthouse and sprint over just as soon as there were signs of a verdict.

Not long after ten, one of these fellows in a cloth cap came bolting into the Lamb tavern shouting that the court was to reassemble at a quarter to eleven. The foot-soldiers of the newspapers quickly mobilized themselves, and by ten-thirty the court room was full again, overflowing in fact, the galleries jammed. The police had given up trying to shut the court room doors so another throng crowded at the rear all the way down the steps and into the street. This was the penultimate moment, a nervous droning hubbub. But as soon as the Clerk of the Court announced a verdict had been agreed, all this noise abruptly stopped. So when John White Webster was led in, he was faced with a sea of staring silent eyes.

The jury came in and took, it seemed to everyone, an age shuffling to their seats; after them and with equal ponderousness the bench.

From the Clerk: 'Gentlemen of the Jury have you reached a verdict?'

Three or four voices replied in a low tone, as if in a church response: 'We have.'

'Who shall speak for you?'

'The Foreman.'

'John W. Webster, hold up your right hand! Foreman look upon the prisoner! What say you, Mr Foreman, is John W. Webster the prisoner at the bar, guilty or not guilty?'

Byram the locksmith hesitated just a moment, as though there might yet be an alternative. 'Guilty.'

'Gentlemen of the Jury, hearken to your verdict as the Court have recorded it. You upon your oaths do say that John W. Webster the prisoner at the bar is guilty: so you say, Mr Foreman, so, Gentlemen say you all.'

The word, then was sounded twice. At its first enunciation, John W. Webster visibly started; his right hand gripped the rail and his head fell. At the second his carriage suddenly gave and his body dropped into the chair.

Nothing moved, no sound was heard. A void had opened and swallowed the room with its hundreds of people and hundreds of thousands of words. Minutes passed this way in terrible immobility. While all eyes were concentrated on the man, his own were covered to avoid meeting them. Even when Counsel went to the bar, murmured something of resources not yet tried, a writ of error, John Webster stayed with his head lowered as if his neck would not bear the weight of it.

At last the Chief Justice managed to break from this paralysis and gave a mute order, with his hand, for the court to be cleared; the clerk barking it out. Men and women began to move off, looking behind them at Webster, still sitting, a handkerchief now over his eyes. Then, in the middle of this foot-dragging, boots creaking against the plank floor, a sound that was half-cry, half-command, like something wounded and ashamed and angry: 'Take me away from this place so that I may not be looked on any longer.'

And so they did; and as if released from some spell, the stuffy room became once more a place of human assembly and disassembly from which each in his own way, at last, went home.

'What a relief it was to us,' wrote one of the jury, the next week, 'when we were again allowed to "go free" and rejoin our families and friends after so long and painful a separation! And there was not a Juror's heart but would have leapt for joy could the prisoner have been justly allowed the same unspeakable blessing.'

7

Great fun, the macabre, as confirmed by brisk sales of Ambrose Bierce and Edgar Allen Poe.

A year before he killed George Parkman, John Webster had organized a little after-supper entertainment at his house. At a signal, the maid lowered the gas lamps. Candles were doused and a bowl of blue phosphorous was brought in, little curls of flame shooting about the glass and throwing unearthly reflections against the walls. Suddenly a shriek came from one of the ladies, for leaning over the bowl, his face livid blue, her host appeared, a rope around his neck, tongue lolling from a corner of the mouth. A huge joke!

April Fools' Day, 1850. Ten past nine in the court-house, Constable Jones and jailer Andrews brought in the prisoner, his wrists in irons, his expression distraught and sick. Every so often and at irregular moments his eyes would shut tight, and when they opened they rolled wildly about the room or at the ceiling.

Confronted with this spectacle of misery it was hard to keep one's composure; indeed for many of the principals in the room, it was quite impossible. One who was not there, the brilliantly acid New York lawyer Abraham Oakley Hall, reading reports of the shedding of tears thought them all 'a blubbering set': Dr Keep crying over his dentures; Littlefield weeping when he found the remains; the jury apparently in tears for over forty minutes before the foreman could get a vote out of them (they had apparently spent another two hours in silent prayer). And this morning, the Attorney-General who went through the form of asking for the 'sentence which the law of this Commonwealth affixes for this offence' and the Chief Justice who passed it both did so with tremulous, lachrymose voices and much dabbing at eyes and cheeks.

Crocodile tears? Listening to the Chief Justice it was difficult to believe so. He began by speaking of 'meeting you [the prisoner] here for the last time' as though they were at a class reunion, and then of the indescribable pain he felt at passing the sentence of death. And then, after going through the conventional summary of the crime and the trial, he lapsed into the voice of the preaching pastor, a mere servant of the Chief of all Justices. On his behalf and sixth commandment, he urged him, should he think his punishment too severe,

> if one repining thought arises in your mind or one
> murmuring word seeks utterance from your lips—think,

oh think of him instantly deprived of life by your guilty
hand; then if not lost to all sense of retributive justice, if
you have any compunctious visitings of conscience you
may perhaps be ready to exclaim, in the bitter anguish
of truth—'I have sinned against Heaven and my own
soul; my punishment is just; God be merciful to me a
sinner.'

There followed more pieties on the terrible example this case
might be, especially to the young, to 'guard against the
indulgence of every unhallowed and vindictive passion.' Yet the
Chief Justice refrained from issuing the usual words of advice
that he freely offered when addressing the more normal species of
cutthroat, as he put it 'the illiterate, the degraded, the outcast,
whose early life has been cast among the vicious . . . who have
been blessed with no means of moral and religious culture, who
have never received the benefits of cultivated society nor enjoyed
the sweet and ennobling influences of home.' In such a case as
this, 'where all the circumstances have been reversed,' he need not
act the moral tutor. The Professor could take his own lessons to
heart.

What he was to declare was the voice of the law. Yet God
forbid he should make this merely an official act and not express
his sympathy and compassion, 'and though we have no word of
present consolation or earthly hope to offer you in this hour of
your affliction, we devoutly commend you to the mercy of our
Heavenly Father with whom is abundance of mercy and from
whom we may all hope for pardon and peace!'

With what seemed a great effort, the words of the sentence
were uttered: 'Removed from this place . . . close custody . . .
thence taken at such time . . . to the place of execution there to
be hung by the neck.'

Another immense silence broken again by sounds from the
prisoner's dock; a soft, sobbing lamentation; his forehead fallen
abruptly against the bar.

To leave the place he needed two men to support him with
their arms, just as he had four months before on the night of his
arrest. Outside the court the crowd surged towards him shouting,

and he ducked spontaneously as though they might hurt him with their cries and then, with a strength drawn from somewhere unknown, sprinted like a schoolboy to the waiting police carriage.

8

No legal proceedings could shake the faith of the Webster family in the unblemished innocence of the Professor. When the Prescotts had brought the news of the verdict out to Garden Street the morning following the trial, Mrs Webster had been so paralysed with horror that she could say nothing; Marianne had thrown herself into a wild keening and the other girls had crumpled in sobbing misery. But a resumed indignation at the injustice that had been done together with a resolution to help their afflicted father did something to revive them. With a diminishing circle of faithful friends—Charles Cunningham, the Prescotts, Fanny Longfellow—they brought the Doctor comforts: baked goods from home; some lavender water. Webster's junior counsel, Ned Sohier, brought cigars. He busied himself with an intensive reading programme and preparing his own petition of pardon.

There were signs, too, that should all else fail, Webster was attending to his spiritual welfare. Towards the end of May he had begun regular conversations with a minister of the Unitarian Church in Roxbury, George Putnam. On the twenty-third of that month, George Parkman's remains were taken from the vault beneath Trinity Church and transferred to Mount Auburn cemetery and in the afternoon the Reverend Putnam spoke with a new firmness to his charge. There was, he said, 'one barrier to our free communication:' the knowledge he must have had about Dr Parkman's fate. The time had now come for it to be shared.

Perhaps, at last, John Webster would tell the truth. Perhaps. For the only version of the confession elicited by George Putnam is the one the minister himself brought to the Governor's Council on Pardons on 2 July. In the meantime, John Webster's own petition for clemency, based on his continuing insistence of innocence, had been withdrawn.

Yet even as related by Putnam, the statement has, in essence, the ring of truth. It narrated the harassment for debt; the appointment with Dr Parkman made so that Webster could implore him for more time, for the sake of the family. When he arrived on the Friday afternoon

> he called me a liar and a scoundrel and heaped upon me the most opprobrious epithets and taunts. As he shouted at me he drew the two notes for the money I owed him and an old letter from Dr Hosack, a letter in which Dr Hosack congratulated Dr Parkman on getting me appointed as a professor of chemistry.
>
> 'I got you into your position and now I will get you out of it!'
>
> I cannot tell how long the torrent of threats and invectives continued. I cannot begin to recall all that Dr Parkman said to me in those moments. At first I kept trying to interject comments in the hope of pacifying him, but I could not stop him and soon my own anger was aroused. At that point I felt nothing but the sting of his words. I grew furious.
>
> While he was speaking and gesturing in the most violent and menacing manner—thrusting Dr Hosack's letter in my face—I seized whatever thing was nearest me, a stick of wood and dealt him a blow with all the force passion could summon. I did not know, nor think nor care where I should hit him nor how hard nor what the effect should be.
>
> He fell to the floor instantly. He did not move.
>
> I knelt beside him. Blood flowed from his mouth and I got a sponge and wiped it away. I got some ammonia and held it to his nose. I spent ten minutes in attempts to resuscitate him but he was dead.
>
> In my horror I ran to the doors and bolted them. A terrible awful panic engulfed me. What should I do?

It never occurred to me to go for help, to tell what had happened. All I could see was the need to conceal Dr Parkman's body in order to avoid the blackest disgrace.

Then followed: dragging the body to the back room, stripping clothes, burning them; removing all his possessions, later throwing a watch over the Craigie bridge; dismembering the corpse with the bowie knife; distributing the parts in different places and cleaning the area to efface the slightest trace of blood.

What had the weapon been? A stump of grapevine that he had brought to the College for an experiment showing how wood could take on the colour of certain chemicals.

The whole deed, terrible as it was, had been entirely unpremeditated. He had picked up the *two* notes without thinking and even more bizarrely pocketed them rather than burned them. If there had been premeditation why should he have called expressly at Parkman's house that morning to make the appointment; why make it for his own premises?

At the end of it all, so he reported, the Reverend Putnam had solemnly asked John Webster—'as a dying man, truthfully'—did he never have a thought that the death of Dr Parkman would be an advantage to him?

'No, never,' he cried. 'As I live and as God is my witness I was no more capable of such a thought than one of my innocent children. I never had the remotest idea of injuring Dr Parkman until the moment the blow was struck. Dr Parkman was extremely severe and sharp-tongued, the most provoking of men, and I am irritable and passionate. A quickness and violence of temper has been the besetting sin of my life. I was an only child, much indulged and I have never acquired the control over my passions that I should have acquired early and the consequence of it all is this.'

Is this it, then, the truth of the case, the ultimate nugget of certainty that historians once imagined they would find if only they looked hard and long enough in the archives? Can a man truly be slain with a stump of grapevine? And what actually was it, this lethal piece of timber? Though the confession initially had it as an item for experimental demonstration, Webster had added a 'supplemental note' in which he changed his mind and said all the grapevines had been brought to the College to be burned for ash that would fertilize his garden. Ashes to ashes.

Can a man be killed *instantaneously* with a blow from a piece of wood? Impossible, said one set of doctors who came to testify to the Council; quite possibly, if not likely, said another set, citing the fragility of the temples and Dr Parkman's particularly brittle cranial structure.

But just think of this man, said members of the Council. Think of what we know by his own admission: such a creature as this managed to play whist, go to evening parties, read Milton, give lectures, carve the Thanksgiving turkey, even as he was mutilating and burning, forging a letter and concocting an abominable deception. Would such a monster as this not hesitate to lie once more if he thought it would rescue him from the gallows?

No, think rather of his family, said just one other member of the Council, Benjamin Goode. Three days after the first hearing Mrs Webster had appeared dressed in mourning black before the committee, along with all three daughters. Her face, below the black lace, was wet with tears; the girls struggling bravely to bear the immense weight of their anguish.

On 19 July, Lieutenant-governor Reed gave Governor George Briggs notice that with only one dissenting vote the committee had voted to reject the petition for clemency.

9

Not that he is of high degree
We ask you him to save
Not that he is a useful man
Pardon for him we crave
Not that his virtuous loving wife
Still unto him doth cling

And feels that she would part with life
From death to rescue him
Not that three lovely daughters plead
With many a bitter tear
And humbly look to God and you
To save their father dear
But save him O for justice's sake
And for our country's fame
The honor of the Commonwealth
And for your own good name

My own good name! What do I care for that, thought the Governor. Just give me my horse and my chickens and keep reputation. But the poem is really quite commendable in its sentiments. And it scans, more or less: *dee-da-dee-da-dee-da-dee-da.* He opened a box labelled 'Petitions', unwrapped the pink ribbon and set the verses on top of others whose contents and authors he knew by heart, for there wasn't a day when he didn't peruse them, however crazy or illiterate.

Some like Mr Pearce of Fayetteville in North Carolina pleaded insanity, for he couldn't imagine how someone could both premeditate a murder (as convicted) and call at the victim's house to solicit an interview on a day of public lectures and not be manifestly demented.

Then there were those, in their different fashions, who were militantly opposed to capital punishment. Charles Spear, the leader of the campaign, had asked the Governor for a stay until further petitions could be brought. And he had granted it, and to be sure they had come from New Hampshire, Connecticut, New York, but not in such overwhelming numbers—still less with overpowering reasons—to set aside the execution. To all the philosophico-ethical passions mustered in those arguments he still preferred the simple soul who had asked him 'to take care of his Disconsolate Wife and Daughters and know that hanging him don't fetch the dead to life.'

With that he had, alas, no quarrel. He wasn't even sure, if the matter were ever to come to a vote, how he would decide, for his Baptist God was, variously, a stern Jehovah and a forgiving

Redeemer. But he was, or had been, like almost all those in politics, a man of the law and the statute was the statute. Nothing in the record of the trial, not the fiercest provocation offered by George Parkman, he thought, could make this anything other than a murder for which the penalty was unequivocally prescribed.

Well, the task, however loathsome, was his; he could not evade it.

Perhaps, next year, I shall be set free, he thought. And something inside George Briggs made a little jump, like the trout clearing the surface of the Housatonic.

He reached for his pen.

10

29 August 1850. A conspiracy of silence had been organized between the Reverend George Putnam, Sheriff Eveleth and John Webster to keep the execution date from Harriet and the girls. Putnam, who was not a sentimental man (quite the opposite in fact), was impressed by this last act of unselfishness on the condemned man's part. The minister liked to think of himself as the instrument of a true atonement, a pastor who had shown a pathetic sinner the way to redemption—who could say, perhaps even to Paradise?

He had already made some amends. In the court room, he had publicly repudiated his own counsel and had insisted on addressing the jury directly himself. He had now written to his senior defence counsel to ask forgiveness for this act of churlishness. With his junior counsel Ned Sohier, who visited many times a week and who showed the sincerest concern for his family, he knew he need not make any formal apology. He understood the desperation that had caused him to offend in such a way; but better he seemed to understand the horrible flux that had made him into a raving brute. It had been, he now knew, a chemical alteration. The word that came to his mind over and again was *ebullition*. How many times had he used it in his lectures when discussing the boiling point of liquids or the reaction of acids and alkali. That had been the rage in his blood, a foaming bubbling turmoil that forced its way over the rim of his vessel and scalded whatever was in its way.

Images of glass bottles with vehemently frothing fluids came into his mind; himself standing before the students explaining as best he could in the midst of their boyish noisiness; more images, this time line engravings in the pages of his child's history book, of Vesuvius in eruption pouring lava down on to sinful Herculaneum below. More images still, of himself with a stick raised against a college friend, frantic with hatred that he had lost a game of tipping the hat; worse, later, waving a razor against a man who had joked at a barbershop that he had never seen a monkey shaved!

Why had no one told him before, someone versed in these matters of mental disorder, that that was what he suffered from: periodic attacks of *ebullition*? Oh, he knew it was an old-fashioned term, gone out of favour, but who knew its scientific precision better than he? The Erving Professor of Chemistry had had the property of being changed, chemically, from good to evil. Now the process would be reversed, this time metaphysically.

There had been so much time. Now there seemed so little. He wondered how his letter of sorrow and contrition, addressed to Francis Parkman, had been received. He had tried, even at the trial, to hold out his hand to him but knew it would not be taken. He knew too, that of all that family, it was the churchman who perhaps was most adamant that he be punished to the letter of the Hebraic law. Well he could understand that too; he hoped only to make him understand the truth, that until his brother began the persecution, he had felt nothing but gratitude to him. Would he ever comprehend that?

If there were one thing more he would have wished for it was a little solitude. But orders had been given, usual for these occasions, he understood, never to leave a condemned man by himself. Even at this minute Mr Andrews was sitting on his stool at the other end of the cell reading *The Transcript*. What would be said about him on the morrow, he wondered? Nothing so cruel it would lacerate his poor bereft girls?

A
h, of all the deceitful countenances he had contrived these last months, the hardest was this very evening. They had brought him dried flowers from Fayal whose scent had called him back to that blessed island, some of his favourite *nougat de Montelimar* and a volume of Longfellow's verses. The necessary charade almost broke down when Mr Andrews told him there was a crowd gathering on Leverett Street and he thought the news had become public after all. But the good-hearted jailer had made up some story about a load of fuel being delivered and invited them to leave through his quarters instead.

At another moment, too, he thought *they* must somehow have known, though there was nothing on their faces to show it. For by some small miracle they had reached, in their daily readings of the Gospel, Corinthians, I: 15.

And when Marianne reached the passage that began, 'O death, where is thy sting, O grave thy victory?' he had rested his chin on the dark head of his little Catherine, and a great stream of tears had fallen on her crown.

11

30 August 1850. A delectable summer night in Boston, velvety warmth and the stars hanging like studs in the blackness.

All the afternoon, as it became known that John Webster had been hanged at the jail, crowds—immense and sometimes unruly—had gathered in front of the gates at Mount Auburn cemetery. It had been the condemned man's wish to be interred there, and the newspapers had duly reported this. Cambridge had never seen such traffic. After carriages had dropped some folks off by the cemetery gates, they took others for a drive about the Common to catch a glimpse of the murderer's house; to marvel at the apparent ordinariness. How could black-eyed Susans grow in such profusion about a place stained by sin and crime?

But no hearse, nor nothing like it, nor even a suspiciously laden cart ever appeared. Even so, some who insisted that it would arrive under cover of darkness, settled down to spend the night if need be, in anticipation of the thrilling moment.

No one was looking for a wagon with a coffin hidden aboard going in quite the other direction, away from Leverett Street, down towards the docks and north to Copps Hill. Ned Sohier's son and a pleasant boy called Will drove the horse, neither too slowly nor too quick, the hooves clattering on the cobbles. Close to the path, half-way up the hill, there was a space amid the stones. The jailer Mr Andrews set a dim lamp by it and the three men dug as fast as they could, lumps of turf flying against the moonlit sky. When they had done Ned Sohier paused for a moment on his shovel, his whole body hot and wet with the work. Were his fellow-beings so truly abandoned that they had to go through this elaborate subterfuge to avoid the desecration of a grave? He remembered what John Webster had told him about Ephraim Littlefield. That he had never doubted. The possibilities sent a shiver through his frame.

Together the men lifted the heavy box towards the hole. For a second, Mr Andrews lost his footing, sending the coffin swinging sharply to Ned Sohier. To keep his balance and prevent it from falling, he found himself embracing the upright box, his cheeks pressed against the roughly planed wood for a full minute, before the others helped him, very gently, to lower it into the dirt.

The author is grateful to the archivists of the Harvard University Archives and the Massachusetts Historical Society for invaluable help in researching this story.

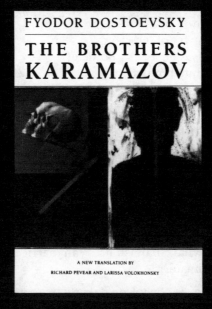

WILLIAM BOYD
CORK

M y name is Lily Campendonc. A long time ago I used to live in Lisbon.

I lived in Lisbon between 1929 and 1935. A beautiful city, but melancholy.

Boscán, Christmas 1934: 'We never love anyone. Not really. We only love our idea of another person. It is some conception of our own that we love. We love ourselves, in fact.'

'Mrs Campendonc?'

'Yes?'

'May I be permitted to have a discreet word with you? Discreetly?'

'Of course.'

He did not want this word to take place in the office so we left the building and we walked down the rua Serpa towards the Arsenal. It was dark, we had been working late, but the night was warm.

'Here, please. I think this small café will suit.'

I agreed. We entered and sat at a small table at the rear. I asked for a coffee and he for a small glass of *vinho verde*. Then he decided to collect the order himself and went to the bar to do so. While he was there I noticed him drink a brandy standing at the bar, quickly, in one swift gulp.

He brought the drinks and sat down.

'Mrs Campendonc, I'm afraid I have some bad news.' His thin, taut features remained impassive. Needlessly he restraightened his straight bow-tie.

'And what would that be?' I resolved to be equally calm.

He cleared his throat, looked up at the mottled ceiling and smiled vaguely.

'I am obliged to resign,' he said, 'I hereby offer you one month's notice.'

I tried to keep the surprise off my face. I frowned. 'That *is* bad news, Senhor Boscán.'

'I am afraid I had no choice.'

'May I ask why?'

'Of course, of course, you have every right.' He thought for a while, saying nothing, printing neat circles of condensation on the tan scrubbed wood of the table with the bottom of his wine glass.

'The reason is . . .' he began, 'and if you will forgive me I will be entirely candid—the reason is,' and at this he looked me in the eye, 'that I am very much in love with you, Mrs Campendonc.'

Cork

'The material of which this monograph treats has become of double interest because of its shrouded mystery, which has never been pierced to the extent of giving the world a complete and comprehensive story. The mysticism is not associated with its utility and general uses, as these are well known, but rather with its chemical make-up, composition and its fascinating and extraordinary character.'

Consul Schenk's Report on the Manufacture of Cork, Leipzig 1890

After my husband, John Campendonc, died in 1932 I decided to stay on in Lisbon. I knew enough about the business, I told myself, and in any event could not bear the thought of returning to England and his family. In his will he left the company—the Campendonc Cork Company Ltd.—to me with instructions that it should continue as a going concern under the family name or else be sold. I made my decision and reassured those members of John's family who tried earnestly to dissuade me that I knew exactly what I was doing, and besides there was Senhor Boscán who would always be there to help.

I should tell you a little about John Campendonc first, I suppose, before I go on to Boscán.

John Campendonc was twelve years older than me, a small strong Englishman, very fair in colouring, with fine blond hair that was receding from his forehead. His body was well muscled with a tendency to run to fat. I was attracted to him on our first meeting. He was not handsome—his features were oddly lopsided—but there was a vigour about him that was contagious, that characterized his every movement and preoccupation. He read vigorously, for example, leaning forward over his book or newspaper, frowning, turning and smoothing down the pages with a flick and crack and a brisk stroke of his palm. He walked everywhere at high speed and his habitual pose was to thrust his left hand in the pocket of his coat—thrust strongly down—and, with his right hand, to smooth his hair back in a series of rapid caresses. Consequently his coats were always distorted on the left, the pocket bulged and baggy, sometimes torn, the constant strain on the seams inevitably proving too great. In this manner he wore out three or four suits a year. Shortly before he died I found a tailor in the rua Garrett who would make him a suit with three identical coats. So for John's fortieth birthday I presented him with an assortment of suits—flannel, tweed and cotton drill—consisting of three pairs of trousers and nine coats. He was very amused.

I retain a strong and moving image of him. It was about two weeks before his death and we had gone down to Cascaes for a picnic and a bathe in the sea. It was late afternoon and the beach was deserted. John stripped off his clothes and ran naked into the sea, diving easily through the breakers. I could not—and still cannot—swim and so sat on the running-board of our motor car, smoked a cigarette and watched him splash about in the waves. Eventually he emerged and strode up the beach towards me, flicking water from his hands.

'Freezing,' he shouted from some way off. 'Freezing freezing freezing!'

This is how I remember him, confident, ruddy and noisy in his nakedness. The wide slab of his chest, his fair, open face, his thick legs darkened with slick wet hair, his balls clenched and shrunken with cold, his penis a tense white stub. I laughed at him and pointed at his groin. Such a tiny thing, I said, laughing. He stood there, hands on his hips, trying to look offended. Big enough for you, Lily Campendonc, he said, grinning, you wait and see.

Two weeks and two days later his heart failed him and he was dead and gone forever.

Why do I tell you so much about John Campendonc? It will help explain Boscán, I think.

'The cork tree has in no wise escaped from disease and infections; on the contrary it has its full allotted share which worries the growers more than the acquiring of a perfect texture. Unless great care is taken all manner of ailments can corrupt and weaken fine cork and prevent this remarkable material from attaining its full potential.'

Consul Schenk's Report

Agostinho da Silva Boscán kissed me one week after he had resigned. He worked out his month's notice scrupulously and dutifully. Every evening he came to my office to report on the day's business and present me with letters and contracts to sign. On this particular evening, I recall, we were going over a letter of complaint to a cork grower in Elvas—hitherto reliable—whose cork planks proved to be riddled with ant borings. Boscán was standing beside my chair, his right hand flat on the leather top of the desk, his forefinger slid beneath the upper page of the letter ready to turn it over. Slowly and steadily he translated the Portuguese into his impeccable English. It was hot and I was a little tired. I found I was not concentrating on the sonorous monotone of his voice. My gaze left the page of the letter and focused on his hand, flat on the desk top. I saw its even, pale brownness, like milky coffee, the dark glossy hairs that grew between the knuckles and the first joint of the fingers, the nacreous shine of his fingernails . . . the pithy edge of his white cuffs, beginning to fray . . . I could smell a faint musky perfume coming off him—farinaceous and sweet—from the lotion he put on his hair, and mingled with that his own scent, sour and salt . . . His suit was too heavy, his only suit, a worn shiny blue serge, made in Madrid he had told me, too hot for a summer night in Lisbon . . . Quietly, I inhaled and my nostrils filled with the smell of Agostinho Boscán.

'If you say you love me, Senhor Boscán,' I interrupted him, 'why don't you do something about it?'

'I am,' he said, after a pause. 'I'm leaving.'

He straightened. I did not turn, keeping my eyes on the letter.

'Isn't that a bit cowardly?'

83

William Boyd

'Well,' he said. 'It's true. I would like to be a bit less . . .
cowardly. But there is a problem. Rather a serious problem.'
    Now I turned. 'What's that?'
    'I think I'm going mad.'

My name is Lily Campendonc, *née* Jordan. I was born in Cairo
in 1908. In 1914 my family moved to London. I was educated
there and in Paris and Geneva. I married John Campendonc in
1929 and we moved to Lisbon where he ran the family's cork
processing factory. He died of a coronary attack in October 1931.
I had been a widow for nine months before I kissed another man,
my late husband's office manager. I was twenty-four years old
when I spent my first Christmas with Agostinho da Silva Boscán.

The invitation came, typewritten on a lined sheet of cheap writing
paper.

> My dear Lily,
>   I invite you to spend Christmas with me. For three
> days—24, 25, 26 December—I will be residing in the
> village of Manjedoura. Take the train to Cintra and
> then a taxi from the station. My house is at the east end
> of the village, painted white with green shutters. It
> would make me very happy if you could come, even for
> a day. There are only two conditions. One, you must
> address me only as Balthazar Cabral. Two, please do
> not depilate yourself—anywhere.
>   Your good friend,
>   Agostinho Boscán

'Balthazar Cabral' stood naked beside the bed I was lying in.
His penis hung long and thin, but slowly fattening, shifting.
Uncircumcised. I watched him pour a little olive oil into the palm
of his hand and grip himself gently. He pulled at his penis,
smearing it with oil, watching it grow erect under his touch. Then
he pulled the sheet off me and sat down. He wet his fingers with
the oil again and reached to feel me.
    'What's happening?' I could barely sense his moving fingers.

'It's an old trick,' he said. 'Roman centurions discovered it in Egypt.' He grinned. 'Or so they say.'

I felt oil running off my inner thighs on to the bed clothes. Boscán clambered over me and spread my legs. He was thin and wiry, his flat chest shadowed with fine hairs, his nipples were almost black. The beard he had grown made him look strangely younger.

He knelt in front of me. He closed his eyes.

'Say my name, Lily, say my name.'

I said it. Balthazar Cabral. Balthazar Cabral. Balthazar Cabral . . .

'After the first stripping the cork tree is left in the juvenescent state to regenerate. Great care must be taken in the stripping not to injure the inner skin or epidermis at any stage in the process, for the life of the tree depends on its proper preservation. If injured at any point growth there ceases and the spot remains for ever afterward scarred and uncovered.'

Consul Schenk's Report

I decided not to leave the house that first day. I spent most of the time in bed, reading or sleeping. Balthazar brought me food— small cakes and coffee. In the afternoon he went out for several hours. The house we were in was square and simple and set in a tangled, uncultivated garden. The ground floor consisted of a sitting-room and a kitchen and above that there were three bedrooms. There was no lavatory or bathroom. We used chamber-pots to relieve ourselves. We did not wash.

Balthazar returned in the early evening bringing with him some clothes which he asked me to put on. There was a small short cerise jacket with epaulettes but no lapels—it looked vaguely German or Swiss—a simple white shirt and some black cotton trousers with a draw-string at the waist. The jacket was small, even for me, tight across my shoulders, the sleeves short at my wrists. I wondered if it belonged to a boy.

I dressed in the clothes he had brought and stood before him as he looked at me intently, concentrating. After a while he asked me to pin my hair up.

'Whose jacket is this?' I asked as I did so.

'Mine,' he said.

We sat down to dinner. Balthazar had cooked the food. Tough stringy lamb in an oily gravy. A plate of beans the colour of pistachio. Chunks of greyish spongy bread torn from a flat crusty loaf.

On Christmas Day we went out and walked for several miles along unpaved country roads. It was a cool morning with a fresh breeze. On our way back home we were caught in a shower of rain and took shelter under an olive tree, waiting for it to pass. I sat with my back against the trunk and smoked a cigarette. Balthazar sat cross-legged on the ground and scratched designs in the earth with a twig. He wore heavy boots and coarse woollen trousers. His new beard was uneven—dense around his mouth and throat, skimpy on his cheeks. His hair was uncombed and greasy. The smell of the rain falling on the dry earth was strong—sour and ferrous, like old cellars.

That night we lay side by side in bed, hot and exhausted. I slipped my hands in the creases beneath my breasts and drew them out, my fingers moist and slick. I scratched my neck. I could smell the sweat from my unshaven armpits. I turned. Balthazar was sitting up, one knee raised, the sheet flung off him, his shoulders against the wooden headboard. On his side of the bed was an oil-lamp set on a stool. A small brown moth fluttered crazily around it, its big shadow bumping on the ceiling. I felt a sudden huge contentment spill through me. My bladder was full and was aching slightly, but with the happiness came a profound lethargy that made the effort required to reach below the bed for the enamel chamber-pot prodigious.

I reached out and touched Balthazar's thigh.

'You can go tomorrow,' he said. 'If you want.'

'No, I'll stay on,' I said instantly, without thinking. 'I'm enjoying myself. I'm glad I'm here.' I hauled myself up to sit beside him.

'I want to see you in Lisbon,' I said, taking his hand.

'No, I'm afraid not.'

'Why?'

'Because after tomorrow you will never see Balthazar Cabral again.'

'From this meagre description we now at least have some idea of what "corkwood" is and have some indication of the constant care necessary to ensure a successful gathering or harvest, while admitting that the narration in no wise does justice to this most interesting material. We shall now turn to examine it more closely and see what it really is, how this particular formation comes about and its peculiarities.'

Consul Schenk's Report

Boscán: 'One of my problems, one of my mental problems, rather—and how can I convince you of its effect?—horrible, horrible beyond words—is my deep and abiding fear of insanity . . . Of course, it goes without saying: such a deep fear of insanity is insanity itself.'

I saw nothing of Boscán for a full year. Having left my employ he became, I believe, a free lance translator, working for any firm that would give him a job and not necessarily in the cork industry. Then came Christmas 1933, and another invitation arrived, written on a thick buff card with deckle edges in a precise italic hand, in violet ink:

Senhora Campendonc,
    Do me the honour of spending the festive season in my company. I shall be staying at the Avenida Palace Hotel, rooms 35–38, from the 22–26 December inclusive.
Your devoted admirer,
J. Melchior Vasconcelles
PS: Bring many expensive clothes and scents. I have jewels.

Boscán's suite in the Avenida Palace was on the fourth floor. The bellhop referred to me as Senhora Vasconcelles. Boscán greeted me in the small vestibule and made the bellhop leave my cases there.

Boscán was dressed in a pale grey suit. His face was thinner, clean-shaven, and his hair was sleek, plastered down on his head with Macassar. In his shiny hair I could see the stiff furrows made from the teeth of the comb.

When the bellhop had gone we kissed. I could taste the mint from his mouthwash on his lips.

Boscán opened a small leather suitcase. It was full of jewels, paste jewels, rhinestones, strings of artificial pearls, *diamanté* brooches and marcasite baubles. This was his plan, he said: this Christmas our gift to each other would be a day. I would dedicate a day to him, and he to me.

'Today you must do everything I tell you,' he said. 'Tomorrow is yours.'

'All right,' I said. 'But I won't do everything you tell me to, I warn you.'

'Don't worry, Lily, I will ask nothing indelicate of you.'

'Agreed. What shall I do?'

'All I want you to do is to wear these jewels.'

The suite was large: a bathroom, two bedrooms and a capacious sitting-room. Boscán/Vasconcelles kept the curtains drawn, day and night. In one corner was a free-standing cast-iron stove which one fed from a wooden box full of coal. It was warm and dark in the suite; we were closed off from the noise of the city; we could have been anywhere.

We did nothing. Absolutely nothing. I wore as many of his cheap trinkets as my neck, blouse, wrists and fingers could carry. We ordered food and wine from the hotel kitchen which was brought up at regular intervals, Vasconcelles himself collecting everything in the vestibule. I sat and read in the electric gloom, my jewels winking and flashing merrily at the slightest shift of position. Vasconcelles smoked short stubby cigars and offered me fragrant oval cigarettes. The hours crawled by. We smoked, we ate, we drank. For want of anything better to do I consumed most of a bottle of champagne and dozed off. I woke, fuzzy and irritated, to find that Vasconcelles had drawn a chair up to the sofa I was slumped on and was sitting there, elbows on knees, chin on fists, staring at me. He asked me questions about the business, what I had been doing in the last year, had I enjoyed my trip home to England, had the supply of cork from Elvas improved and so on. He was loquacious, we talked a great deal but I could think of nothing to ask him in return. J. Melchior Vasconcelles was, after all, a complete stranger to me and I sensed it would put his tender personality under too much strain to inquire about his circumstances and the fantastical life he led. All the same, I was very curious, knowing Boscán as I did.

'This suite must be very expensive,' I said.

'Oh yes. But I can afford it. I have a car outside too. And a driver. We could go for a drive.'

'If you like.'

'It's an American car. A Packard.'

'Wonderful.'

That night when we made love in the fetid bedroom he asked me to keep my jewels on.

'It's your turn today.'

'Thank you. Merry Christmas.'

'And the same to you . . . What do you want me to do?'

'Take all your clothes off.'

I made Vasconcelles remain naked for the entire day. It was at first amusing and then intriguing to watch his mood slowly change. Initially he was excited, sexually, and regularly aroused. But then, little by little, he became self-conscious and awkward. At one stage in the day I watched him filling the stove with coal, one-handed, the other hand cupped reflexively around his genitals, like the adolescent boys I had once seen jumping into the sea off a breakwater at Cidadella. Later still he grew irritable and restless, pacing up and down, not content to sit and talk out the hours as we had done the day before.

In mid afternoon I put on a coat and went out for a drive, leaving him behind in the suite. The big Packard was there, as he had said, and a driver. I had him drive me down to Estoril and back. I was gone for almost three hours. When I returned Vasconcelles was asleep, lying on top of the bed in the hot bedroom. He was deeply asleep, his mouth open, his arms and legs spread. Some more agitated movement had caused his penis to be thrown across his left thigh exposing his scrotum, oddly dark, wrinkled like a peach stone, a soft purse resting on the bedspread. His chest rose and fell slowly and I saw how very thin he was, his skin stretched tight over his ribs. When I looked closely I could see the shiver and bump of his palpitating heart.

Before dinner he asked me if he could put on his clothes. When I refused his request it seemed to make him angry. I reminded him of our gifts and their rules. But to compensate him I wore a tight sequinned gown, placed his flashy rings on my fingers and roped imitation pearls round my neck. My wrists ticked and clattered with preposterous rhinestone bangles. So we sat and ate: me, Lily Campendonc, splendid in my luminous jewels and, across the table, J. Melchior Vasconcelles, surly and morose, picking at his Christmas dinner, a crisp linen napkin spread modestly across his thighs.

'The various applications of cork that we are now going to consider are worthy of description as each application has its *raison d'être* in one or more of the physical or chemical properties of this marvellous material. Cork possesses three key properties that are unique in a natural substance. They are: impermeability, elasticity and lightness.'

Consul Schenk's Report

I missed Boscán after this second Christmas with him, much more—strangely—than I had after the first. I was very busy in the factory that year—1934—as we were installing machinery to manufacture Kamptulicon, a soft, unresounding cork carpet made from cork powder and indiarubber and much favoured by hospitals and the reading rooms of libraries. My new manager—a dour, reasonably efficient fellow called Pimentel— saw capably to most of the problems that arose but refused to accept responsibility for any but the most minor decisions. As a result I was required to be present whenever something of significance had to be decided, as if I functioned as a symbol of delegatory power, a kind of managerial chaperone.

I thought of Boscán often, and many nights I wanted to be with him. On those occasions, as I lay in bed dreaming of Christmas past and, I hoped, Christmas to come, I thought I would do anything he asked of me—or so I told myself.

One evening at the end of April I was leaving a shop on the rua Conceição, where I had been buying a christening present for my sister's second child, when I saw Boscán entering a café, the Trinidade. I walked slowly past the door and looked inside. It was cramped and gloomy and there were no women clients. In my glimpse I saw Boscán lean eagerly across a table, around which sat half a dozen men, and show them a photograph, which they at first peered at, frowning, and then breaking into wide smiles. I walked on, agitated, the moment fixed in my mind's eye. It was the first time I had seen Boscán, and Boscán's life, separate from myself. I felt unsettled and oddly envious. Who were these men? Friends or colleagues? I wanted suddenly and absurdly to share in that moment of the offered photograph, to frown and then grin conspiratorially like the others.

I waited outside the Trinidade sitting in the back seat of my motor car with the windows open and the blinds down. I made Julião, my old chauffeur, take off his peaked cap. Boscán eventually emerged at about seven-forty-five and walked briskly to the tramway centre at the Rocio. He climbed aboard a No.2 which we duly followed until he stepped down from it near São Vicente. He set off down the steep alley-ways into the Mouraria. Julião and I left the car and followed him discreetly down a series of *boqueirão*—dim and noisome streets that lead down to the Tagus. Occasionally there would be a sharp bend and we would catch a glimpse of the wide sprawling river shining below in the moonlight, and beyond it the scatter of lights from Almada on the southern bank.

Boscán entered the door of a small decrepit house. The steps up to the threshold were worn and concave, the tiles above the porch were cracked and slipping. A blurry yellow light shone from behind drab lace curtains. Julião stopped a passer-by and asked who lived there. Senhor Boscán, he was told, with his mother and three sisters.

'Mrs Campendonc!'

'Mr Boscán.' I sat down, opposite him. When the surprise and shock began to leave his face I saw that he looked pale and tired. His fingers touched his bow-tie, his lips, his ear lobes. He was smoking a small cigar, chocolate brown, and wearing his old blue suit.

'Mrs Campendonc, this is not really a suitable establishment for a lady.'

'I wanted to see you.' I touched his hand, but he jerked it away as if my fingers burned him.

'It's impossible. I'm expecting some friends.'

'Are you well? You look tired. I miss you.'

His gaze flicked around the café. 'How is the Kamptulicon going? Pimentel is a good man.'

'Come to my house. This weekend.'

'Mrs Campendonc . . .' His tone was despairing.

'Call me Lily.'

He steepled his fingers. 'I'm a busy man. I live with my mother and three sisters. They expect me home in the evening.'

'Take a holiday. Say you're going to . . . to Spain for a few days.'

'I only take one holiday a year.'

'Christmas.'

'They go to my aunt in Coimbra. I stay behind to look after the house.'

A young man approached the table. He wore a ludicrous yellow overcoat that reached down to his ankles. He was astonished to see me sitting there. Boscán looked even iller as he introduced us. I have forgotten his name.

I said goodbye and went towards the door. Boscán caught up with me.

'At Christmas,' he said quietly. 'I'll see you at Christmas.'

A postcard. A sepia view of the Palace of Queen Maria Pia, Cintra:

> I will be one kilometre west of the main beach at Paco d'Arcos. I have rented a room in the Casa de Bizoma. Please arrive at dawn on 25 December and depart at sunset.
>
> I am your friend,
Gaspar Barbosa

'The bark of the cork tree is removed every 8–10 years, the quality of the cork improving with each successive stripping. Once the section of cork is removed from the tree the outer surface is scraped and cleaned. The sections—wide curved planks—are flattened by heating them over a fire and submitting them to pressure on a flat surface. In the heating operation the surface is charred, and thereby the pores are closed up. It is this process that the industry terms the "nerve" of cork. This is cork at its most valuable. A cork possesses "nerve" when its significant properties—lightness, impermeability, elasticity—are sealed in the material for ever.'

Consul Schenk's Report

In the serene, urinous light of dawn the beach at Paco d'Arcos looked slate grey. The seaside cafés were closed up and conveyed sensations of dejection and decrepitude as only out-of-season holiday resorts can. To add to this melancholy scene, a fine cold rain blew off the Atlantic. I stood beneath my umbrella on the coast road and looked about me. To the left I could just make out the tower of Belem. To the right the hills of Cintra were shrouded in a heavy opaque mist. I turned and walked up the road towards the Casa de Bizoma. As I drew near I could see Boscán sitting on a balcony on the second floor. All other windows on this side of the hotel were firmly shuttered.

A young girl, of about sixteen years, let me in and led me up to his room.

Boscán was wearing a monocle. On a table behind him were two bottles of brandy. We kissed, we broke apart.

'Lise,' he said. 'I want to call you Lise.'

Even then, even that day, I said no. 'That's the whole point,' I reminded him. 'I'm me—Lily—whoever you are.'

He inclined his body forward in a mock bow. 'Gaspar Barbosa . . . Would you like something to drink?'

I drank some brandy and then allowed Barbosa to undress me, which he did with pedantic diligence and great delicacy. When I was naked he knelt before me and pressed his lips against my groin, burying his nose in my pubic hair. He hugged me, still kneeling, his arms strong around the backs of my thighs, his head turned sideways in my lap. When he began to cry softly I raised him up and led him over to the narrow bed. He undressed and we climbed in, huddling up together, our legs interlocking. I reached down to touch his penis, but it was soft and flaccid.

'I don't know what's wrong,' he said. 'I don't know.'

'We'll wait.'

'Don't forget you have to go at sunset. Remember.'

'I won't.'

We made love later but it was not very satisfactory. He seemed listless and tired—nothing like Balthazar Cabral or J. Melchior Vasconcelles.

At noon—the hotel restaurant was closed—we ate a simple lunch he had brought himself: bread, olives, tart sheep's milk cheese, oranges and almonds. By then he was on to the second bottle of brandy. After lunch I smoked a cigarette. I offered him one—I had noticed he had not smoked all day—which he accepted but which he extinguished after a couple of puffs.

'I have developed a mysterious distaste for tobacco,' he said, pouring himself more brandy.

In the afternoon we tried to make love again but failed.

'It's my fault,' he said. 'I'm not well.'

I asked him why I had had to arrive at dawn and why I had to leave at sunset. He told me it was because of a poem he had written, called 'The Roses of the Gardens of the God Adonis'.

'You wrote? Boscán?'

'No, no. Boscán has only written one book of poems. Years ago. These are mine, Gaspar Barbosa's.'

'What's it about?' The light was going; it was time for me to leave.

'Oh . . .' He thought. 'Living and dying.'

He quoted me the line which explained the truncated nature of my third Christmas with Agostinho Boscán. He sat at the table before the window, wearing a dirty white shirt and the trousers of his blue serge suit and poured himself a tumblerful of brandy.

'It goes like this—roughly. I'm translating: "Let us make our lives last one day," he said. "So there is night before and night after the little that we last."'

'The uses to which corkwood may be put are unlimited. And yet when we speak of uses it is only those that have developed by reason of the corkwood's own peculiarity and not the great number it has been adapted to, for perhaps its utility will have no end and, in my estimation, its particular qualities are but little appreciated. At any rate it is the most wonderful bark of its kind, its service has been a long one and its benefits, even as a stopper, have been many. A wonderful material truly, and of interest, so full that it seems I have failed to do it justice in my humble endeavour to describe the Quercus Suber of Linnaeus—Cork.'

Consul Schenk's Report

Boscán, during, I think, that last Christmas: 'You see, because I am nothing, I can imagine *anything* . . . If I were something, I would be unable to imagine.'

It was early December 1935 that I received my last communication from Agostinho Boscán. I was waiting to hear from him as I had received an offer for the business from the Armstrong Cork Company, and was contemplating a sale and, possibly, a return to England.

I was in my office one morning when Pimentel knocked on the door and said there was a Senhora Boscán to see me. For an absurd, exquisite moment I thought this might prove to be Agostinho's most singular disguise, but I remembered he had three sisters and a mother still living. I knew before she was shown in that she came with news of Boscán's death.

Senhora Boscán was small and tubby with a meek pale face. She wore black and fiddled with the handle of her umbrella as she spoke. Her brother had specifically requested that I be informed of his death when it arrived. He had passed away two nights before.

'What did he die of?'

'Cirrhosis of the liver . . . He was . . . My brother had become an increasingly heavy drinker. He was very unhappy.'

'Was there anything else for me that he said? Any message?'

Senhora Boscán cleared her throat and blinked. 'There is no message.'

'I'm sorry?'

'That is what he asked me to say: "There is no message."'

'Ah.' I managed to disguise my smile by offering Senhora Boscán a cup of coffee. She accepted.

'We will all miss him,' she said. 'Such a good, quiet man.'

From an obituary of Agostinho da Silva Boscán:

'. . . Boscán was born in Durban, South Africa in 1888 where his father was Portuguese consul. He was the youngest of four children, the three elder being sisters. It was in South Africa that he received a British education and learned to speak English. Boscán's father died when he was seventeen and the family returned to Lisbon, where Boscán was to reside for the rest of his life. He worked primarily as a commercial translator and office manager for various industrial concerns, but mainly in the cork business. In 1916 he published a small collection of poems, *Insensivel*, written in English. The one Portuguese critic who noticed them, and who wrote a short review, described them as 'a sad waste'. Boscán was active for a while in Lisbon literary circles and would occasionally publish poems, translations and articles in the quarterly review *Sombra*. The death of his closest friend, Xavier Quevedo, who committed suicide in Paris in 1924, provoked a marked and sudden change in his personality which became increasingly melancholic and irrational from then on. He never married. His life can only be described as uneventful . . .'

JAN BOGAERTS
CHRISTMAS IN BAVARIA

B ergtesgaden was, for some time, the home town of both Adolf Hitler and Dieter Eckhardt, the father of national socialism. It is a small place in Bavaria not far from the Austrian border. I did not live through the last war, but I was interested in seeing if there was something about this particular place that could have created two such men.

I stayed there for a short time over Christmas. I was not made welcome. The people objected to me photographing them. They made it clear that they did not like to have an outsider at their celebrations. Despite the fact that the Wall had just come down this was a very introspective community. While they rejected the past of Hitler they were very firm in their belief of their own traditions; very protective and assured of their particular cultural identity. The sense of this being a time and a place for families was *very* strong.

At Christmas time in Bergtesgaden the young men dress up as monsters and are licensed to hit people, any people, with whips. This was a form of absolution. I was hit a couple of times, hard, and it hurt for a long time afterwards.

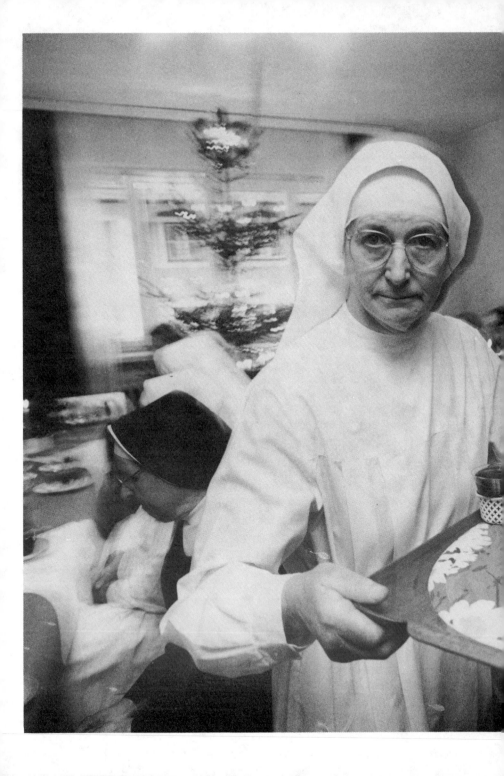

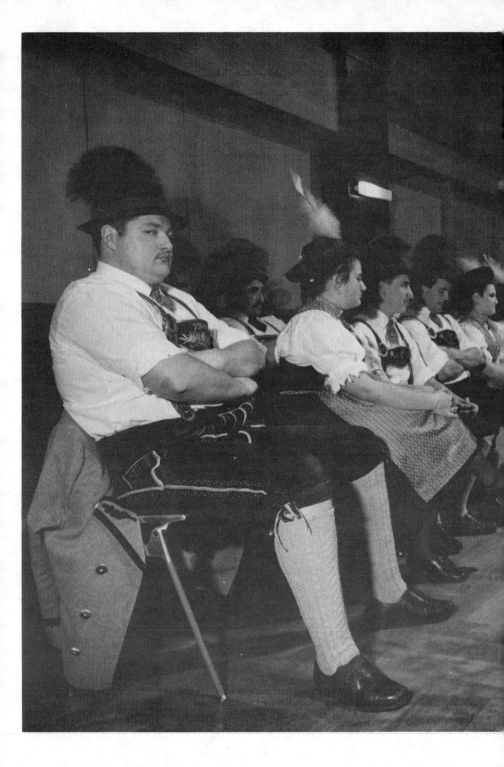

GEOFFREY WOLFF
THE GREAT SANTA

What a moody cuss He was. Manic-depressive doesn't tell the half of it; recollect His haphazard night-time unloading of His Christmas Eve cargo at my place: an Omega wrist-watch in my stocking that year, a lump of coal the next. The Great Santa, like circumstance itself, blew hot and cold; He was all caprice, chance, crapshoot. Christmas charts the wobbly course of the American Family Wolff, going to and fro on the continent, up and down the greasy pole. When we had a chimney, He slid down it. When we had a roof, He might land on it. So here's how Christmas past was for us, and how it was unforeseen.

Upside: of Noel, yuletide cheer, good will toward man, mistletoe, holly, the wreath, the candy-cane, a sugar-dust of snow, sleigh bells, Dancer Prancer and Blixen, Tiny Tim, the roast turkey and cooked goose—Speak, memory! Let me jiggle recall's little glass paperweight and watch the snowflakes spread, settling on an ear-muffed cub with wool mittens clipped to his snowsuit; he's dragging a sled. A blue spruce is tied to the sled and a collie pup, Shep, races circles around the boy and the boy's freight, burying his muzzle in the powdery flakes. Mom and Dad are giggling, tossing loosely packed, talcumy snowballs at each other. In yonder red-barnboarded farmhouse (with all modern appliances, copper pipes, and wired to code), carollers are rehearsing. Mom and Dad and Shep and little Jeffie pause to cock an ear to 'Hark the Herald Angels Sing' and 'Good King Wenceslas'. Dad—not one teensy bit tipsy—pours hot buttered rum from a battered stainless steel thermos; the good cheer steams atmospherically from a mug.

'Merry Christmas, dear,' he says.

'And Merry Christmas to you, honey,' says Mom, her eyes misting from a near-excess of warm feeling.

And they, in unison, 'Merry Christmas, Jeff.'

Shep, wagging his tail, barks.

Utterly allegorical, right off memory's Hallmark card. Let me deal from a straight deck. My mother was a lapsed Irish Catholic, my father an unacknowledging Jew, the son of an atheist surgeon. My mother was pretty as a picture, with dreamy blue eyes and an appetite for adventure. My father was bright, quick, musical, charming, a wonderful story-teller. He was also a bullshit artist

Opposite: Geoffrey Wolff with his parents.

who doctored his blood-line and fabricated his curriculum vitae, becoming the man he felt he should have been rather than the man his history had made. I heard it said of him (at an age when I thought the reference was to pets) that he could weave a pussy out of steel wool. His chosen field of work was aircraft engineering, and he was good at it, bogus academic degrees notwithstanding. Such a family as mine is not designed for constancy, but my single persistent expectation growing up was that Christmas would by Jesus be celebrated. My father loved to buy on credit, and he relished giving even more than getting.

1941

Farmington, Connecticut. Pre-Christmas at the Elm Tree Inn. For gift-oriented celebrants of Christ's birthday these weeks pre-Christmas are more memorable than those post-. So it is that I recall 7 December so clearly. Father is in England, selling P-51s, Mustangs, to the British, Lend-Lease. Mother and I have been batting aimlessly around the country in a new Packard convertible, and this morning she is in the bath-tub and I am listening to the radio. I give her the news through the bathroom door that the Japanese have bombed Pearl Harbor. I am four; she doesn't believe me, but in the excitement of the moment forgets to remove from the bath-tub the gift she has been test-driving under the suds, a wind-up submarine bought at the toystore F.A.O. Schwarz which is, like the rest of America, on a war footing. I remember all this because of the sub, a well-made and satisfying contraption, my first memory provoked by pleasure rather than by having a heavy Packard door shut on my thumb.

 *

---

*Note to the reader: I assay my experience of the Holy Birthday according to the convention established by Michelin in its

1944

Birmingham, Alabama. In an oversized, columned and ersatz ante-bellum house across the golf course from the Mountain Brook Country Club I'm hanging around the edges of a Christmas Eve party of airplane designers, draftsmen, test pilots, model-makers, gunsmiths, expediters, grease monkeys—can-do men and women, performers. This is a company party; my dad is chief engineer of an airplane modification enterprise that installs state-of-the-art bomb-sights, ordnance, armour, navigational equipment; the improved B-17 Flying Fortresses and B-24 Liberators and (later) B-29 Super Fortresses will be returned by ferry pilots to India or Guam or England, wherever the action's hot. Time is life in war, and the pressure on these improvers to perform is measurable even to a squirt like moi-même; there's nervous static in this room. The crowd's impatient, noisy and raffish, and my father's in their midst, making them laugh. He's telling stories I don't understand; I just turned seven.

I'm especially attracted to this one of our many house guests. He's a carrier-based dive-bombing pilot who was shot down over Rabal and escaped the evil, dread Nips by wooden raft. Now he's a ferry pilot, delivering bombers from Birmingham to the Pacific Theater. He's got up as Santa Claus, the skinny devil. 'Ho, ho, ho, my young flyboy. And what would you like to find under the tree tomorrow morning?' I think I still believe in the second-story man and chimney sweep, but I know who this is under the beard, wearing dark glasses, drinking Fish House Punch through a bent glass straw. The pilot's face, awfully burned, has been poorly repaired; that face is the first strangeness I have come to take for granted. His face isn't what interests me. What interests me: his

judgement of eating and sightseeing and resting facilities. The quality and quantity of gifts received (by me) is bestowed one to four 'Santas'. What I call quality of life (Was an edible holiday feast dinner served in a timely manner? Did we live in a house with a fireplace? With a separate bedroom for me? Was snow on the ground? Was the snow clean? Was Daddy shit-faced?) I rate with 'Frosty the Snowman' (or men), one to four.

railroad empire of HO gauge model trains he has set up in our basement. My God, what a dream of a world he has contrived: Alpine villages with sheep and goats and cows by the tracks; tunnels, city terminals; bizarre, loopy cross-overs so intricately knotted that I can't credit the hairbreadth escape of the tightly timed trains vying for right of way. Oh: the locomotives whistle, blow steam. So what do I hope to find under the tree tomorrow? Puh-leeze.

I remember that night, after the party, spying atavistically from the landing. ('I Saw Mommy Kissing Santy Claus'? Not yet, not this Christmas. My mother tonight looks swell in an Auxiliary Red Cross uniform, nipped at the waist, a dove grey worsted flattering to her curly blonde hair.) I witness the tinkerers and wizards of electronics and hydraulics defeated by *my* little Lionel and its single, symmetrical oval, until they aren't, until they puzzle it out. I remember too the next morning when some hungover bully-boys of last night's revels, horsing around with my own toy train, pour too many watts to its transformer, till it derails. But what I value of this memory is not the electric train but an atmosphere of competence in the house where I live. This is not an illusion. Around me everyone is busy, working and having fun. It is comforting to have people milling around with matters of more moment than Christmas and me on their minds. I am not starved for attention or affection. I am already, at seven, overfed on attention, fat on affection.

1945

New York City. *Pacem in terris,* alas for the Wolffs. Dad's been sacked. Now I've got a baby brother, cute as a pin, but his diapers are washed in the toilet we share with a Dane (who fills the ice-box with his stash, a block of dope as big as his head—personal use only), and with a turbaned Sikh jazz freak, and with the Dane's wife, who's Everyman's friend (but not Everywoman's, not my mom's—the diapers, I guess); she's a la-di-dah childhood pal of my dad's, and now an editor of *The Daily Worker*. The tenement *ménage* is a walk-up two-bedroom railroad flat on East 57th, under the rumbling shadow of the Third Avenue El. Theatrically squalid, a crib, a damned manger, for Christ's sake. Dad looks for work, sort of, and drinks Black Horse Ale, paid for by the trust fund communist. Christmas Eve they listen to 78s of Fats Navarro and Bird and Pres. 'Silent Night' my ass! There's a squabble among the communards, sparked by obscure tinder, division of labour. As I now understand, the to-eaches (from the trust fund) got out of synch with the from-eaches (to the Wolffs). The dispute's flared by my father's prudish, condemning judgement of reefer (which the flat-sharers call 'mary-jane'). Could Dad have had hold already of the concept of ambient smoke? Whatever, the fight spills over; I get my first whipping ever for eavesdropping through the door. What door? I don't know yet but I'll know soon how to listen for the special music of my father's voice when spirits take him, when good cheer glooms him, when the o'er-brimming wassail cup drowns his sweetness. It's a trombonish sound, whiny but deep, long-playing, as welcome as an announcement from Herod that he's been thinking about babies.

  (I got Lincoln Logs.)

No Frosties

1946

Saybrook, Connecticut. Ground-zero bottomed-out misery. My father, hero of the Super Fortress soup-up center, is engaged in the manufacture of a fishing device he has co-invented and co-patented with another childhood friend, a would-be capitalist.

The thingumajig is a red flag at the end of a steel spring mounted on a balsa square which floats on the surface of the water. From this bobbing platform descends fishing line, sinker, bait, hook. When the fish bites (which it doesn't), the flag unsprings (which it doesn't). A modification calls for the end of the flag-rod to ring a bell, but this makes the gizmo top-heavy, and it capsizes. As I well know. When the ice melts a little on the Connecticut River, I am the invention's test pilot. We live in two tiny rooms of a boarding house, a bona fide flea-bag with genuine fleas. Our fellow tenants are old geezers limping down the home stretch; they walk their towel-racks down the narrow, dark hallways, whispering our name: 'Have the Wolffs paid their rent yet?' 'I bet the Wolffs haven't paid their re-yent yet.' 'Throw the bums out in the snow, they haven't paid their ray-yent.' 'Why should we have to pay our rent when the Wolffs haven't paid their rahyay-ent yet?' 'They never pay their rent, the Wolffs . . . '

No Santas
No Frosties

1947

Old Lyme, Connecticut. Dad got a job, 'bought' a farmhouse (with the co-signature on the mortgage deed of another childhood well-to-do but ne'er-did-well). Noel will never look prettier. Here's the allegorical yule-tide scene, the Holy Birthday avatar. Here's the collie Shep, the snow, the wool mackinaw, the earmuffs, the pretty country lane. Here's the sled. Here's the sun low in a cobalt sky morning after a sixteen-inch fall of fresh powder. Here I'm belly-down on the new Flexible Flyer at the top of Gin Mill Lane, about to shove off. Here Dad says don't do this, don't go there, don't especially put your tongue against that metal tie-rod. The metal tie-rod tastes OK at first, till I pull my tongue away. The blood tastes salty. It looks pretty, those little rubies set against white. Boy oh boy, another screwed-up Christmas morning, a Wolff Xmas avatar. The night before had started out OK, till Dad fell into the tree, after the chimney fire burned out, after eating the well-done meat. Doesn't everyone cook steak in the fireplace? Over logs? Soaked in gasoline?

(Before Christmas Eve dinner)

(Before the Sled)

No Frosties   *(In Dr Von Glaun's office)*

1948

Old Lyme, Connecticut. Singing 'O Come, All Ye Faithful' in Miss Champion's fifth grade homeroom, standing behind M------t D--n, kissing like a sneak-thief her copper hair, growing a micro-chubby in my cuffed bluejeans—will I burn in hell, oh ye faithful? 'Angels We Have Heard on High.' I'll say. I buy her older brother a Gilbert chemistry set. I've never exchanged a word with him, but I spend my Christmas allowance on a Gilbert chemistry set. I deliver it to him in sixth grade, tell him to tell her to love me. OK, OK: what would you have done?

Dad consoles me in the bar of New London's Mohegan Hotel, where we celebrate having bought the best tree ever. He's up, high. Every year, every tree, best tree ever. Sweet calculus, who can fault it? The bartender mis-speaks, calls Dad 'baldy' or 'buddy' or 'pal' or 'Duke', which is his name. It doesn't matter what the bartender calls him or says. At a certain point that I can now recognize, the score calls for the trombone. His voice slides down the scale, and we leave the bar, or rather we are asked to leave. Someone—bartender or Daddy—says, 'I don't have to listen to that shit on Christmas Eve.' Such words are being spoken in bars up and down the Christian world on this holy night. 'Fuck you, buddy, and the horse you rode in on.' Driving home in the '37 Ford station wagon, the old man shows me how to steer out of a skid, almost. Our hides are OK, and while we wait in the cold front seat, in the shallow ditch, for the tow-truck called by the merry Christmasers who have managed so to incense my father (with their 'patronizing' invitation to have a seat and wait in their warm living-room till the truck comes) that he fuck-yous them . . . While my dad has a free moment with me, he shares some observations he's recently made. He stares at me as though he's never noticed me before, and I think then maybe he hasn't. I don't feel this coming, this time. From tonight I'll never not feel it coming, when I hear the trombone tuning. 'Well, you're really something, aren't you? You're quite a number, don't you know? You never weary of kicking me in the ass, do you? You're bleeding me white. You're really something, aren't you?' (*Repeat chorus.*)

But: next morning there are sacks-full of stuff. Stuffed stocking hanging from the mantel, stuffed clumsily wrapped boxes, heavy with promise, an erector set, a Gilbert 'Atomic' chemistry set in a metal travelling case, turkey with walnut stuffing. Also: apologies, let me make it up to you, how would you like a Raleigh bicycle, a Remington single-shot .22? I say I'd like them fine.

C hristmas was my father's specialty season: it sanctioned impulse buying, excess, radical behaviour, time out from work, lies. At Christmas I had my first inkling how dearly my father loved to lie. 'Oh, we're so broke!' (This was true.) 'Oh, please understand, there can't be any presents this year.' Sure. The only doubt was, where had he hidden them? Christmas called for deceit right down the line: bogus information on the charge account application, a sham pre-inventory of the cornucopia that awaited discovery under the tree, a misleading presentation of the booty (camera wrapped in a box suited for a basketball). And, of course, the gifts were hidden. My mother always hid them on the top shelf of her closet, in hat-boxes. My father went to extreme ends to protect his secrets: a drug mule couldn't take greater pains. I never found what he had stashed. Forget the attic, the mud-floored cellar. In Old Lyme I fished in an abandoned well, looking for the loot. I levered a manhole cover off our cesspool. Wherever the goods were, I wasn't.

1949

Sarasota, Florida. Father is in Istanbul, on the lam from the creditors who paid for our re-done farmhouse, his sports car, my Christmas presents. He has been working the Bazaar; he entrusts a flow of exotic oddities to my mother's safekeeping. We—also in flight from those creditors—live in a moist, beaver-boarded cabin on Siesta Key. The floor-board splinters can penetrate thick-soled black Keds. The tap-water stinks of sulphur. There's a store-room back of the hovel, and this is where the stuff from Turkey is stored. What will fit in hat-boxes is in hat-boxes, of course. The ceremonial Turkish sword is under a blanket. Or its hilt is. About a foot of blade is in plain sight. This is careless hiding; like a clock striking thirteen, such desultory deception upsets my sense of the order of things and makes me a little crazy. My pathology expresses itself in unintended parody of my old man's over-extended conduct. I stockpile my allowance, steal change and small bills from my mom's purse. I study the Sears catalogue, accumulate Christmas presents for my mother. These are of such a stunning inappropriateness—a sun hat, costume jewellery, a heavy wool blanket, a cheapjack redwood chest in which to hide the tawdry crap—that even then I must have known that this venture was bent. In downtown Sarasota—where I cruise for goods to half-hide from my mother, merchandise with which wholly to surprise her, stun her, overwhelm her—the sun blazes unwholesomely. Forget snow, we're greased with Coppertone. Tin stars and rubber angels hang forlornly from the overhead power lines and I hum along to 'Rudolph the Red-Nosed Reindeer' and 'Frosty the Snowman'. (Has 'Jingle Bell

Rock' yet been composed? If so, that too.) For Mom, I steal a Christmas card, another allegory, a fuzzy simulacrum of our Old Lyme *tableau vivant* (snow, pup, tyke, sled, perfect little tree). It is ornate, and stinks of lavender cologne. 'Too much of a muchness,' in the oft repeated formulation of my stepmother.

My soon to be stepmother, rather. My rich stepmother, by Santa! My at-first-generous stepmother. My elderly stepmother. My under-certain-misapprehensions-about-my-father's-history-and-prospects stepmother.

1952

Boston. Holy smoke, a suite at the Ritz Carlton. I've got a privileged, unimpeded view of Boston Public Garden. We dine in the second-floor dining room. A dinner-jacketed and evening-dressed double quartet carols us with 'God Rest You Merry, Gentlemen' and 'Away in a Manger'. Master Wolff wears rather a handsome flannel suit. It's a well-made garment, the flannel neither too charcoalish nor too pale, the tailoring unobtrusively unpinched at the waist, the trousers unpleated (but cuffed, of course), the ensemble unwaistcoated. It shows off to advantage my necktie, deep purple with the gold arms of the Choate School, *quae sivi bona tibi*, we seeke to do thee goode, which I have already learned to translate: 'we seek to do thee: good.' Oh-oh. My father and stepmother have selected my new flannel suit on Newbury Street from Brooks Brothers, where a Chesterfield coat has been exhibited in a display window, with snowflakes applied to its rich wool shoulders and rich velvet collar. 'It looks like dandruff,' I'd said. Oh, dear, this kind of thing is about to become a problem. Just what Christmas needs, another wisenheimer.

I fly to Sarasota to visit my mother. She works in a Dairy Queen. The night after Christmas her middle-aged boyfriend tries to break down the tiny basement apartment's only door, to get at her. We sit in silence, pretending not to be there. My mother gives me an ivory-plastic table radio with a dial lit as mystery green as the middle depths of a tropical sea. Getting into my

Don't miss out on major issues.

Every issue of Granta features politics, polemic, travel writing, fiction and more. So don't miss out – subscribe today and save up to 31%.

Name _____

Address _____

_____

_____ Postcode _____

BI341

Please enter my subscription for: ☐ Four issues £19.95

☐ Eight issues £37   ☐ Twelve issues £49.95

Please start my subscription with issue number _____

Payment: ☐ Cheque enclosed

☐ Access/American Express/Visa/Diners Club

Expiry date _____

☐☐☐☐☐☐☐☐☐☐☐☐☐☐☐☐

Signature

_____

Overseas postage: Europe: Please add £6 per year. Outside Europe: £12 per year air-speeded, £20 per year airmail.

Please tick this box if you do not want to receive direct mail from other companies ☐

UP TO 31% OFF

Give Granta this Christmas.

A subscription to Granta makes a perfect gift and it's so easy to arrange! Just complete and return the form and we'll do the rest, sending your greetings directly to the recipient.

Your Name _____

Address _____

_____

_____ Postcode _____

BI342

Please send a subscription to Granta, with my compliments, to:

Recipient's Name _____

Address _____

_____

_____ Postcode _____

Four issues of Granta at £19.95, starting with issue number _____

If copies are going overseas, for Europe add £6.00; outside Europe, add £12.00 for Air Speeded delivery, or £20.00 for Air Mail.

Payment: ☐ Cheque enclosed

☐ Access/American Express/Visa/Diners Club

Expiry date: _____

☐☐☐☐☐☐☐☐☐☐☐☐☐☐☐☐

Signature

_____

Please tick this box if you prefer not to receive direct mail from other companies ☐

GRANTA

NO
STAMP
REQUIRED

GRANTA Subscriptions
FREEPOST
3/4 Hardwick Street
London EC1R 1TR

NO
STAMP
REQUIRED

GRANTA Subscriptions
FREEPOST
3/4 Hardwick Street
London EC1R 1TR

father's new Jaguar at Boston airport, I drop it, and it breaks. My father promises to replace it with a better radio. This, for a wonder, does not console me.

(Sarasota)

(Boston)

No Frosties   (Sarasota)

1954

The Choate School; Wallingford, Connecticut. The evening before vacation begins. In the Hill House dining hall, the Reverend Seymour St John intones grace most gracefully, with a tone of assurance that what we are about to eat is not one calorie less than we deserve; we tuck into roast beef with Yorkshire pudding, fruitcake and plum pudding after. Then we go to chapel. I sing baritone in the choir, and put my whole heart into Handel's 'Hallelujah' chorus. After Christmas, back in my room, packing for the three-week jamboree ahead, I essay to entertain my roommate. Now, at last, I wasn't born yesterday, I'm wise to the hustle. I monologue him with a riff I've practised on myself, my best audience: 'Face it, we're talking a plug-ugly baby, aren't we? Can we agree on this much? Tinted, rouged, lipsticked, as pink as boiled ham, pudgy little tits. Jesus! Even the masters—I don't know, Bellini, Tintoretto, Rubens, all those—couldn't make that boy cute. *Putti*, no? Doesn't even have a baby face! Frowning like a wrinkled old codger. And why should His Little Self be merry? How about those gifts? *Jeepers, Kings, just what I've always wanted, Frankincense! Myrrh!* I mean, do you know what myrrh is? It's a spiny shrub, I looked it up. Merry Christmas! And how about those carols, blaring from loudspeakers and rasping tinnily from the vents of elevators, as welcome as 'Happy Birthday' at the next table in an expensive restaurant. And tinsel strung from phone poles, and the Salvation

Army putting the arm on you, and Santa Claus darting into an alley to take a hit off a pint bottle in a paper bag, before he robs the bank of its Christmas Club deposits. No wonder it's the suicide season.'

My roommate says: 'Huh?'

I confuse him, confound myself. Because I'm as soft as a baby too. What I'm soft for is a soft, satiny back beneath my sweaty hand at a fancy-dress ball. A soft breast against my fluttery heart. Soft snow falling past the softly lit street lamps of Park Avenue, looking from uptown down, to Grand Central. A Checker Cab sliding softly past the Central Park South entrance to the Plaza, where I'm about to foxtrot to waltz time (because my stepmother came along too late to have me educated at dancing school, but just in time to lever me on to The List). I'm on The List! I get invited to the Hols, Cols, Gets & Mets (Holiday Ball, Collegiate Dance, Get Togethers, Metropolitan Ball). I've managed, against all odds, to become a junior popinjay, parlour snake, tailor's dummy. I'm training my pipes to drawl Long Island lockjaw. I meet she whom I escort Under the Clock at the Biltmore, where we show off our glad rags. I leave after the dance with another and take her to Jimmy Ryan's, where Wilbur and Sidney DeParis and their Dixieland Ramblers play 'Tannenbaum, O Tannenbaum'; Oh, Christmas Tree. I weep like a baby at the beauty of it all, the satin dresses, satin notched collar on my dinner jacket, satin breasts. At the fresh green Christmas tree smell. At the feel of greenbacks, bux. I weep from nostalgia at the moment just before feeling the feeling that provokes nostalgia. No, I wasn't born yesterday; I was born sixteen years and about 340 days before yesterday. I'm growing old! Boo hoo. Or is that rye and ginger priming my tear's pump?

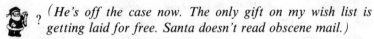 *(He's off the case now. The only gift on my wish list is getting laid for free. Santa doesn't read obscene mail.)*

130

From now until I became a dad Christmas was a calendar reference point rather than a wizard rite. Mother was remarried, and living in places unknown (to the greater world as well as to me; these were places of baroque obscurity, unimaginably uninviting). Father dwelt in a place called trouble and sometimes in prison. I lived hereafter a providentially orphaned life, spending Christmas with foster moms and foster dads, the parents of friends from my schools and universities. I received predictably handsome gifts from these generous people, a Pringle cashmere sweater (or rather sweaters, two, on successive years, from successive benefactors, the first navy, the second tan), a ski sweater, a cableknit tennis sweater; the good people must have thought I was chilly. I was grateful, of course, but I also felt uncomfortable with these families' alien customs. The Philadelphians opened their gifts on Christmas Eve, the Bostonians didn't stoop to drape their tree with the tacky foil icicles the Wolffs (the original, pre-stepmother Wolffs) so favoured. And why roast lamb rather than beef or fowl? And why oh why oh why did my friends' dads' milk-punch-oiled voices on Christmas Eve ascend to the clarinet's register, shrill and nervous and jokey, rather than trombone down where serious sounds are reprised?

When my wife and I were first married we lived in Washington in a perfectly precious little triplex. We had coarse replicas of her parents' and grandparents' furniture bought on the instalment plan. We had oriental rugs and wedding-present hunting prints and wedding-present floral lampshades; we burned pretty little birch logs—more expensive by the cord than dollar bills—in our pretty little fireplace with its pretty little black marble mantel. I wore a suit and tie to Christmas Eve dinner, and during dinner we drank toasts to ourselves and our similarly dressed friends, appropriate wine in apropos glasses. Our tree was decorated, most tastefully, with apt baubles bought from Georg Jensen. We exchanged suitable gifts: from Gucci and Pucci for her, from Cartier for me. The next morning, waking with a wine and port and cognac hangover, with a shoebox-full of bills, I felt puke-sick. Since then, for a quarter century now, we have had the Christmas willies. So we prefer Thanksgiving. But that doesn't

Geoffrey Wolff

mean we crawl into our bomb shelter December 1st and hunker down till after the New Year. We have sons. We buy them stuff.

Writers have the good luck to have bad luck be good luck; the worse the humiliation or fuck-up, the better, the funnier story. Christmas stories are different. They're phenomenal rather than exemplary, nutty rather than extreme. To recollect Christmas is—for me, am I weird here?—to experience a little *frisson* of shame. There's all that crap I craved from Santa, all my feverish gimme. And there's national shame, too: I am a native and citizen of a country in whose greatest metropolis New Yorkers spent Christmas Eve upon Christmas Eve watching on their television sets the slow, oh *so* slow, burning of Hizzoner's Yule Log at Gracie Mansion. These television receivers would be nine-inch Muntz black-and-whites, fuzzed with static, with snow (if you follow my drift).

So maybe our self-loathing, that most American of diseases, sent us packing abroad so many Christmases. In the hills above the south coast of Spain, in Mijas, we lived in a stone house with tile floors that looked and felt like genuine linoleum. That was one cold house, and we heated it with olive logs more fire-proof than asbestos, and about as easy on the lungs when the wind blew smoke at us. Nevertheless, this was a grand establishment, and we had a gardener (who cut the wood and laid the flame-retardant fire) and a cook. We had sons to think of, and I cut a tree (our neighbours would have wanted me to thin their garden's landscaping, if they'd been there to ask), a starveling jack pine that was two feet higher than our ceiling. So I trimmed it from the top, and my wife shouted that I was an idiot, just as she shouted at me two years later when another ceiling was two or three feet too low. The tree's weeping branches were biased to the left, to leeward, as though blasted by the hurricane that howled on Christmas night, driving rain against our rattling picture window. And there came a banging on that window; a man, Lear-like in his operatic dissatisfaction, pressed his face against the glass. He frightened us; my wife instructed me to send him away. Merry Christmas! I found him at our back door; he was a Scot, by Christ, a lad of fifty, stinking of piss and *sangría,* stubbled with cactus prickles, tricked out in a kilt. 'I'm pissed, laddie!'

He claimed to have been thrown from a horse, and he wore an Andalusian riding jacket to bump up the odds of such a version's veracity. He needed a ride to town, couldn't walk. 'Send him away,' my wife said. But it was Christmas, so I bundled him into my car, at the bottom of a steep incline. Working the accelerator and clutch, one hand on wheel, other on gearshift, I was without options when that Wee Horseman of the Apocalypse kissed my mouth and groped for my nuts. 'I'll fucking kill you!' I explained. 'But it's Christmas,' he explained, and so it was. Give me Good Friday.

Maybe not. Maybe once more, we'd try again to get it right. Maybe snowy mountains would help, maybe the Spanish coast was geographically undesirable, Christmasly speaking. In the Arlberg, in Lech, at the Gasthof Post on Christmas Eve my wife and I were taken to the most perfect dinner by an elderly Viennese couple and their gorgeous young daughter, whom we had met in Washington. The staff wore dirndls and loden jackets with stag-horn buttons; by the candlelit glow of a huge balsam, we listened to apple-cheeked youngsters sing Austrian carols and hymns. The Viennese couple, who spoke no English, talked to us through their daughter, whose English was idiomatic. They said how great was the honour to offer us hospitality.

We said how excellent was the food, how satisfying the snow falling outside of the Gasthof Post's windows, falling on the steaming backs of horses waiting to pull us home by sleigh.

The Viennese couple said they wished us to have some small gifts to remember them by. For my wife a Hermès scarf, for me a . . . ski sweater.

We said Merry Christmas, this has got to be as good as Christmas gets.

They said yes, isn't it nice, there aren't any Jews at this hotel.

As bad as Christmas gets? Not quite. It got worse, for me at least, in Sint Maarten, but I don't want to get into that. Let me say only that I got cheated, robbed, slicked with jet fuel, ankle-humped by a mongrel dog and I blew a heart valve. My heart's

133

booboo got cut and spliced, but from then on I have been a fellow who needs to keep a weather eye on his blood, on how nicely it clots, on its coagulation factors, on factor IX, on what haematologists call the Christmas factor.

1990

Here or there. We'll have a nice Christmas. We've calmed down now. We'll have a little tree, and our kids will give us something handmade. We'll eat a two-or three-course dinner Christmas Eve, and we'll hang around the kitchen while it's being cooked. No neckties, but we've taken showers and we wear clean shirts. Maybe we've got Christmas music playing, maybe blues. We laugh a lot, and much of what we laugh about are stories of Christmases past. A good story's a hell of a gift.

Louise Erdrich
I'm A Mad Dog Biting Myself For Sympathy

W ho I am is just the habit of what I always was, and who I'll be is the result. This came clear to me at the wrong time. I was standing in a line, almost rehabilitated. Walgreens was the store in downtown Fargo. I had my purchase in my arms, and I was listening to canned carols on the loudspeaker. I was going to buy this huge stuffed parrot with purple wings and a yellow beak. Really, it was a toucan, I was told this later in the tank.

You think you know everything about yourself, how much money it would take, for instance, to make you take it. How you would react when caught. But then you find yourself walking out the door with a stuffed toucan, just to see if getting caught happens again, and it does, though no one stopped me right at first.

My motive was my girl-friend's Christmas present. And it was strange because I did have the money to pay for a present, though nothing very big or elaborate. I thought of Dawn the minute I saw that bird, and wished I'd won it for her at the county fair, though we never went to a fair. I saw myself throwing a half-dozen softballs and hitting every wooden milk jug, or maybe tossing rings. But those things are weighted or loaded wrong and that's another reason. I never could have won this toucan for Dawn, because the whole thing's a cheat in general. So what the hell, I thought, and lifted the bird.

Outside in the street it was one of my favourite kind of days, right there in the drag middle of winter when the snow is a few hard grey clumps and a dusty grass shows on the boulevards. I liked the smell in the air, the dry dirt, the patches of water shrinking and the threat of snow, too, in the gloom of the sky.

The usual rubber-neck turned to look at me. This bird was really huge and furry, with green underneath its floppy wings and fat stuffed orange feet. I don't know why they'd have a strange thing like this in Walgreens. Maybe a big promotion, maybe some kind of come-on for the holiday season. And then the manager yelled at me from the door. I was half-way down the street when I heard him. 'Come back here!' Probably pointing at me, too, though there was no reason, as I stuck out plenty and still more as I began to run.

First I put the bird underneath my arm. But it threw me off

my balance. So I clutched it to my chest; that was no better. Thinking back now I should have ditched it, and slipped off through the alleys and disappeared. Of course, I didn't— otherwise none of all that happened would have happened. I set the bird on my shoulders and held the lumpy feet under my chin and then I bore down, like going for the distance or the gold, let my legs churn beneath me. I leaped kerbs, dodged among old men in long grey coats and babies in strollers, shot up and over car hoods until I came to the railroad depot and, like it was some sort of destination, though it wasn't, I slipped in the door and looked out the window.

A gathering crowd followed with the manager. There was a policewoman, a few local mall-sitters, passers-by. They were stumbling and talking together and making big circles of their arms, to illustrate the toucan, and closing in.

That's when my stroke of luck, good or bad is no telling, occurred. The car drove into the parking lot, a solid plastic luggage rack strapped on its roof. A man and a woman jumped out, late for a connection, and they left the car running in neutral. I walked out of the depot and stood before the car. At that moment, it seemed as though events were taking me somewhere. I opened up the hinges on the plastic rack, stuffed in the bird. No one seemed to notice me. Encouraged, I got in. I put my hands on the wheel. I took the car out of neutral and we started to roll, backed out of the lot. I changed gears, then turned at the crossroads, and looked both ways.

I don't know what you'd do in this situation. I'll ask you. There you are in a car. It isn't yours but for the time being that doesn't matter. You look up the street one way. It's clear. You look down the other, and a clump of people still are arguing and trying to describe you with their hands. Either way, the road will take you straight out of the town. The clear way is north, where you don't know anyone. South, what's there?

I let the car idle.

My parents. It's not like I hate them or anything. I just can't see them. I can close my eyes and form my sister's face behind my eyelids, but not my parents' faces. Where their eyes should meet mine, nothing. That's all. I shouldn't show up at the farm, not with the toucan. Much less the car. I thought a few seconds longer. The bird on the roof. It was for Dawn. You could say she got me into this, so Dawn should get me out. But she didn't live in Fargo anymore, she lived south. She lived in Colorado, which complicated everything later for it meant crossing state lines and all just to bring her that bird, and then another complexity, although at the time I didn't realize, occurred when the woman at the depot, the one who had left the car, appeared very suddenly in the rear-view mirror.

I had just started moving south when I heard a thump from behind. It was so surprising. Just imagine. She was there on the trunk, hanging on as though by magnetics. She reached up and grabbed the hitches on the roof-top luggage rack, got a better grip, and sprawled across the back window. She was a little woman. Through the side-view, I saw her blue heels in the air, the edge of a black coat. I heard her shrieking in an inhuman desperate way that horrified me so much I floored the gas.

We must have gone by everyone fast, but the effect was dreamlike, so slow. I saw the faces of the clump of people, their mouths fall open, arms stretch and grasp as I turned the corner and the woman rolled over and over like a seal in water. Then she flew off the trunk and bowled them before in her rush so they heaped on the ground beneath her. She was in their arms. They laid her down as though she were a live torpedo and kept running after me.

'Scandinavians,' I thought, because my grandmother's one, 'they don't give up the ghost.' I just wanted to yell out, tell them. 'OK, so it's stolen. It's gone! It's a cheap stuffed bird anyhow and I will *park* the car. I promise.'

I started talking to myself. 'I'll check the oil in Sioux Falls. No sweat.' Then the worst thing came about, and all of a sudden I understood the woman with her eyes rearing back in her skull, her little heels pointed in the air. I understood the faces of the people in the group, their blurting voices, 'b...b...baby'.

As from the back seat, it wailed.

I had my first reaction, disbelief. Then I stopped the car. I had taken the scenic route at a fast clip, but I knew the view anyway. I was down near the river and had decided from there I would take 30 and avoid the Interstate, always so well patrolled. I parked and turned around in a frantic whirl. I revolved twice in my seat. And I still couldn't see the baby. I was behind on the new equipment. He sat in something round and firm, shaped like a big football, strapped down the chest and over the waist, held tight by a padded cushion. Above his face there was a little diamond attachment made of plastic, a bunch of keys and plastic balls that dangled out of reach.

I had never seen a child this little before, so small that it was not a child yet. It's face was tiny and dark, almost reddish, or copper, and its fingers, splayed out against its cheeks, were tiny as the feet of a sparrow. There was a bottle of juice in a bag beside it. I put the end in its mouth and it sucked. But it could not hold the bottle. I kept putting the end in its hand, and it wouldn't grasp.

'Oh screw it,' I finally said, and gunned right out of there. Its cry began again and I wished I knew how to stop it. I had to slow down to get through some traffic. Sirens rushed ahead on their way to the Interstate, passing in a squeal which surprised me. This car, this pack on top, I was so obvious. I thought I'd maybe park at the old King Leo's, get out, and run. But then I passed it. I thought it would be better if I got down south around the South Dakota border, or in the sandhills, where I could hide out in cow shelters. So I did go south. Over me the sky was bearing down and bearing down, so I thought now maybe snow would fall. A White Christmas like the music in the drugstore. I knew how to drive in snow and this car had decent tyres, I could feel them. They never lost grip or planed above the road. They just kept rolling, humming, below me, all four in this unified direction, so dull that after some time it all seemed right again.

The baby dropped off, stopped crying. It shouldn't have been there, should it. I had to realize the situation. There was no use in thinking back, in saying to myself, well you shouldn't have stole the damn bird in the first place, because I did do that and then, well as you see, it was like I went along with the arrangement of things as they happened.

Of course, around half-way down there was a smokey waiting, which I knew would happen, but not whether it would be before or behind me. So now my answer came. The officer's car turned off a dirt road and started flashing, started coming at me from the rear. I took it up to eighty and we moved, *moved*, so the frozen water standing in the fields flashed by like scarves and the silver snow whirled out of nowhere, to either side of us, and what rushed up before us was a heat of road and earth.

I was not all that afraid. I never am and that's my problem. I felt sure they would not use their weapons. I kept driving and then, as we took a turn, as we came to a railroad crossing, I remember hearing the plastic roof rack snap open. I looked through the rear-view by reflex, and saw the bird as it dived out of the sky, big and plush, a purple blur that plunged its yellow beak through the windshield and threw the state police off course so that they skidded, rolled over once, came back with such force the car righted itself and sat there in shock.

I kept on going. The pack blew off and I reasoned that now the car was less obvious. I should have thought about that in the first place, but then the bird would not have hatched out and demolished the police car. Just about this time, however, being as the toucan was gone, I began to feel perhaps there was no reason to go on travelling this way. I began to think I would just stop at the nearest farm, leave the car and the baby, and keep hitching south. I began to think if I showed up at Dawn's, even with nothing, on a Christmas Eve, she would not throw me out. She would have to take me, let me stay there, on the couch. She lived with someone now, a guy ten years older than me, five years older than her. By now he had probably taken her places, shown her restaurants and zoos, gone camping in the wilderness, skied. She would know things and I would still be the same person that I was the year before. And I was glad about the toucan, then, which would have made me look ridiculous. Showing up there like a kid in junior high school with a stuffed animal, when her tastes had broadened. I should have sent her chocolates, a little red and green box. I was wishing I had. And then I looked past the road in front of me and realized it was snowing.

It wasn't just like ordinary snow even from the first. It was like that rhyme or story in the second grade, the sky falling and let's go and tell the king. It came down. I thought to myself, *well, let it come down.* And I kept driving. I know you'll say it, you'll wonder, you'll think what about the child in back of him, that baby, only three weeks old, little Mason Joseph Andrews? Because he did have a name and all, but what could I know of that?

I talked to it. I am good at driving in the snow but I need to talk while I'm driving. I'll tell this now, it doesn't matter. I said, 'You little bastard you, what are you doing here!' It was my state of mind. I put the window open. Snow whited out the windshield and I couldn't see the road in front of us. I watched the margin, tried to follow the yellow line which was obscured by a twisting blanket. I was good at this though I needed my concentration, which vanished when he bawled. My ears were full. He roared and I heard the sound as wind, as sounds that came out of its mother. I hit the plastic egg and felt the straps give against it, felt the car give on the road. I swerved into a car's ruts, wove along the dotted yellow, and then under me was snow and still I kept going at a steady pace although the ground felt all hollow and uncertain. The tracks narrowed into one, and then widened, so I suddenly realized this: I had followed a snowmobile trail and now I was somewhere off the road. Immediately, just like in a cartoon, like Dumbo flying and he realizes that he isn't supposed to be up in the air, I panicked and got stuck.

So now I was in awful shape, out there in a field, in a storm that could go on for three more minutes or three more days. I sat there thinking until the baby got discouraged and fell asleep. And get this. It was a white car. Harder to see than ever. And not a bit of this did I ever think or plan for. I couldn't remember what they said in the papers every fall, the advice about what to do when a blizzard hits. Whether to stay on the road, with the car, or set out walking for help. There was the baby. It was helpless, but did not seem so helpless. I know now that I should have left the car run, the heater, but at the time I didn't think. Except I did rip that dangle of toys off its seat and tie it on the aerial when I went out, and I did leave its blankets in there, never took any. I just wrapped my arms around my chest and started walking south.

By not stopping for a minute I lived through the storm, though I was easy to catch after it let up, and froze an ear. All right, you know that baby wasn't hurt anyway. You heard. Cold, yes, but it lived. They asked me in court why I didn't take it along with me, bundled in my jacket, and I say, well it lived, didn't it? Proving I did right. But I know better sometimes, now that I've spent time alone here in Mandan, more time running than I knew I had available.

I think about that boy. He'll grow up, but already I was more to him than his own father because I taught him what I knew about the cold. It sinks in, there to stay, doesn't it? And people. They will leave you, no matter what you say there's no return. There's just the emptiness all around, and you in it, like singing up from the bottom of a well, like nothing else, until you harm yourself, until you are a mad dog just biting yourself for sympathy, because there is no relenting, and there is no hand that falls, and there is no woman come home to take you in her arms.

I know I taught that boy something in those hours I was walking south. I know I'll always be inside him, cold and black, about the size of a coin, maybe, something he touches against and skids. And he'll say, *what is this*, and the thing is he won't know it is a piece of thin ice I have put there, the same as I have in me, which I never asked for any more than he did.

SVETLANA ALEXIYEVICH
BOYS IN ZINC

In 1986 I had decided not to write about war again. For a long time after I finished my book *War's Unwomanly Face* I couldn't bear to see a child with a bleeding nose. I suppose each of us has a measure of protection against pain; mine had been exhausted.

Two events changed my mind.

I was driving out to a village and I gave a lift to a schoolgirl. She had been shopping in Minsk, and carried a bag with chickens' heads sticking out. In the village we were met by her mother, who was standing crying at the garden gate. The girl ran to her.

The mother had received a letter from her son Andrey. The letter was sent from Afghanistan. 'They'll bring him back like they brought Fyodorina's Ivan,' she said, 'and dig a grave to put him in. Look what he writes. "Mum, isn't it great! I'm a paratrooper . . . " '

And then there was another incident. An army officer with a suitcase was sitting in the half-empty waiting-room of the bus station in town. Next to him a thin boy with a crew-cut was digging in the pot of a rubber plant with a table fork. Two country women sat down beside the men and asked who they were. The officer said he was escorting home a private soldier who had gone mad. 'He's been digging all the way from Kabul with whatever he can get his hands on, a spade, a fork, a stick, a fountain pen.' The boy looked up. His pupils were so dilated they seemed to take up the whole of his eyes.

And at that time people continued to talk and write about our internationalist duty, the interests of state, our southern borders. The censors saw to it that reports of the war did not mention our fatalities. There were only rumours of notifications of death arriving at rural huts and of regulation zinc coffins delivered to prefabricated flats. I had not meant to write about war again, but I found myself in the middle of one.

For the next three years I spoke to many people at home and in Afghanistan. Every confession was like a portrait. They are not documents; they are images. I was trying to present a history of feelings, not the history of the war itself. What were people thinking? What made them happy? What were their fears? What stayed in their memory?

The war in Afghanistan lasted twice as long as the Second World War, but we know only so much as it is safe for us to know. It is no longer a secret that every year for ten years, 100,000 Soviet troops went to fight in Afghanistan. Officially, 50,000 men were killed or wounded. You can believe that figure if you will. Everybody knows what we are like at sums. We haven't yet finished counting and burying all those who died in the Second World War.

In what follows, I haven't given people's real names. Some asked for the confidentiality of the confessional, others I don't feel I can expose to a witch-hunt. We are still so close to the war that there is nowhere for anyone to hide.

One night I was asleep when my telephone rang.

'Listen,' he began, without identifying himself, 'I've read your garbage. If you so much as print another word . . . '

'Who are you?'

'One of the guys you're writing about. God, I hate pacifists! Have you ever been up a mountain in full marching kit? Been in an armoured personnel carrier when the temperature's seventy centigrade? Like hell you have. Fuck off! It's ours! It's got sod all to do with you.'

I asked him again who he was.

'Leave it out, will you! My best friend—like a brother he was—and I brought him back from a raid in a cellophane bag. He'd been flayed, his head had been severed, his arms, his legs, his dick all cut off . . . He could have written about it, but you can't. The truth was in that cellophane sack. Fuck the lot of you!' He hung up; the sound in the receiver was like an explosion.

He might have been my most important witness.

Svetlana Alexiyevich

A Wife

'Don't worry if you don't get any letters,' he wrote. 'Carry on writing to the old address.' Then nothing for two months. I never dreamed he was in Afghanistan. I was getting suitcases ready to go to see him at his new posting.

He didn't write about being in a war. Said he was getting a sun-tan and going fishing. He sent a photo of himself sitting on a donkey with his knees on the sand. It wasn't until he came home on leave that I knew he was in a war. He never used to spoil our daughter, never showed any fatherly feelings, perhaps because she was small. Now he came back and sat for hours looking at her, and his eyes were so sad it was frightening. In the mornings he'd get up and take her to the kindergarten; he liked carrying her on his shoulders. He'd collect her in the evening. Occasionally we went to the theatre or the cinema, but all he really wanted to do was to stay at home.

He couldn't get enough loving. I'd be getting ready to go to work or getting his dinner in the kitchen, and he even grudged that time. 'Sit over here with me. Forget cutlets today. Ask for a holiday while I'm home.' When it was time for him to get the plane he missed it deliberately so we would have an extra two days. The last night he was so good I was in tears. I was crying, and he was saying nothing, just looking and looking at me. Then he said, 'Tamara, if you ever have another man, don't forget this.'

I said, 'Don't talk soft! They'll never kill you. I love you too much for them to be able to.'

He laughed. 'Forget it. I'm a big lad.'

We talked of having more children, but he said he didn't want any more now. 'When I come back you can have another. How would you manage with them on your own?'

When he was away I got used to the waiting, but if I saw a funeral car in town I'd feel ill, I'd want to scream and cry. I'd run home, the icon would be hanging there, and I'd get down on my knees and pray, 'Save him for me, God! Don't let him die.'

I went to the cinema the day it happened. I sat there looking at the screen and seeing nothing. I was really jumpy. It was as if I was keeping someone waiting or there was somewhere I had to go. I barely stuck it out to the end of the programme. Looking back, I think that it must have been during the battle.

It was a week before I heard anything. All of that week I'd start reading a book and put it down. I even got two letters from him. Usually I'd have been really pleased—I'd have kissed them—but this time they just made me wonder how much longer I was going to have to wait for him.

The ninth day after he was killed a telegram arrived at five in the morning. They just shoved it under the door. It was from his parents: 'Come over. Petya dead.' I screamed so much that it woke the baby. I had no idea what I should do or where I should go. I hadn't got any money. I wrapped our daughter in a red blanket and went out to the road. It was too early for the buses, but a taxi stopped.

'I need to go to the airport,' I told the taxi-driver.

He told me he was going off duty and shut the car door.

'My husband has been killed in Afghanistan.'

He got out without saying anything, and helped me in. We drove to the house of a friend of mine and she lent me some money. At the airport they said there were no tickets for Moscow, and I was scared to take the telegram out of my bag to show them. Perhaps it was all a mistake. I kept telling myself if I could just carry on thinking he was alive, he would be. I was crying and everybody was looking at me. They put me on a freight plane taking a cargo of sweetcorn to Moscow, from there I got a connection to Minsk. I was still 150 kilometres from Starye Dorogi where Petya's parents lived. None of the taxi drivers wanted to drive there even though I begged and begged. I finally got to Starye Dorogi at two o'clock in the morning.

'Perhaps it isn't true?'

'It's true, Tamara, it's true.'

In the morning we went to the Military Commissariat. They were very formal. 'You will be notified when it arrives.' We waited for two more days before we rang the Provincial Military Commissariat at Minsk. They told us that it would be best if we

came to collect my husband's body ourselves. When we got to
Minsk, the official told us that the coffin had been sent on to
Baranovichi by mistake. Baranovichi was another 100 kilometres
and when we got to the airport there it was after working hours
and there was nobody about, except for a night watchman in his
hut.

'We've come to collect . . . '

'Over there,' he pointed over to a far corner. 'See if that box
is yours. If it is, you can take it.'

There was a filthy box standing outside with 'Senior
Lieutenant Dovnar' scrawled on it in chalk. I tore a board away
from where the window should be in a coffin. His face was in one
piece, but he was lying in there unshaven, and nobody had
washed him. The coffin was too small and there was a bad smell.
I couldn't lean down to kiss him. That's how they gave my
husband back to me. I got down on my knees before what had
once been the dearest thing in the world to me.

His was the first coffin to come back to my home town,
Yazyl. I still remember the horror in people's eyes. When
we buried him, before they could draw up the bands with
which they had been lowering him, there was a terrible crash of
thunder. I remember the hail crunching under foot like white
gravel.

I didn't talk much to his father and mother. I thought his
mother hated me because I was alive, and he was dead. She
thought I would remarry. Now, she says, 'Tamara, you ought to
get married again,' but then I was afraid to meet her eye. Petya's
father almost went out of his mind. 'The bastards! To put a boy
like that in his grave! They murdered him!' My mother-in-law
and I tried to tell him they'd given Petya a medal, that we needed
Afghanistan to defend our southern borders, but he didn't want
to hear. 'The bastards! They murdered him!'

The worst part was later, when I had to get used to the
thought that there was nothing, no one for me to wait for any
more. I would wake up terrified, drenched with sweat, thinking
Petya would come back, and not know where his wife and child
live now. All I had left were memories of good times.

The day we met, we danced together. The second day we went for a stroll in the park, and the next day he proposed. I was already engaged and I told him the application was lying in the registry office. He went away and wrote to me in huge letters which took up the whole page: 'Aaaaargh!'

We got married in the winter, in my village. It was funny and rushed. At Epiphany, when people guess their fortunes, I'd had a dream which I told my mother about in the morning. 'Mum, I saw this really good-looking boy. He was standing on a bridge, calling me. He was wearing a soldier's uniform, but when I came towards him he began to go away until he disappeared completely.'

'Don't marry a soldier. You'll be left on your own,' my mother told me.

Petya had two days' leave. 'Let's go to the Registry Office,' he said, even before he'd come in the door.

They took one look at us in the Village Soviet and said, 'Why wait two months. Go and get the brandy. We'll do the paperwork.' An hour later we were husband and wife. There was a snowstorm raging outside.

'Where's the taxi for your new wife, bridegroom?'

'Hang on!' He went out and stopped a Belarus tractor for me.

For years I dreamed of us getting on that tractor, driving along in the snow.

The last time Petya came home on leave the flat was locked. He hadn't sent a telegram to warn me that he was coming, and I had gone to my friend's flat to celebrate her birthday. When he arrived at the door and heard the music and saw everyone happy and laughing, he sat down on a stool and cried. Every day of his leave he came to work to meet me. He told me, 'When I'm coming to see you at work my knees shake as if we had a date.' I remember we went swimming together one day. We sat on the bank and built a fire. He looked at me and said, 'You can't imagine how much I don't want to die for someone else's country.'

I was twenty-four when he died. In those first months I would have married any man who wanted me. I didn't know what to do. Life was going on all around me the same as before. One person was building a *dacha*, one was buying a car; someone had got a new flat and needed a carpet or a hotplate for the kitchen. In the last war everybody was grief stricken, the whole country. Everybody had lost someone, and they knew what they had lost them for. All the women cried together. There are a hundred people in the catering college where I work and I am the only one who lost her husband in a war the rest of them have only read about in the newspapers. When I first heard them saying on television that the war in Afghanistan had been a national disgrace, I wanted to break the screen. I lost my husband for a second time that day.

A Private Soldier

The only training we got before we took the oath was that twice they took us down the firing-range. The first time we went there they issued us with nine rounds; the second time we all got to throw a grenade.

They lined us up on the square and read out the order: 'You're going to the Democratic Republic of Afghanistan to do your internationalist duty. Anyone who doesn't want to go, take two paces forward.' Three lads did. The unit commander shoved them back in line with a knee up the backside. 'Just checking morale.' They gave us two days' rations and a leather belt, and we were off. Nobody said a word. The flight seemed to take an age. I saw mountains through the plane window. Beautiful! They were the first mountains any of us had ever seen. we were all from round Pskov, where there are only woodlands and clearings. We got out in Shin Dand. I remembered the date: 19 December 1980.

They took a look at me. 'One metre eighty: reconnaissance company. They can use lads your size.'

We went to Herat to build a firing-range. We were digging,

hauling stones for a foundation. I tiled a roof and did some joinery. Some of us hadn't fired a single shot before the first battle. We were hungry the whole time. There were two fifty-litre vats in the kitchen: one for soup, the other for mash or barley porridge. We had one can of mackerel between four, and the label said, 'Date of manufacture, 1956; shelf-life eighteen months.' In a year and a half, the only time I wasn't hungry was when I was wounded. Otherwise you were always thinking of ways to get something to eat. We were so desperate for fruit that we'd slip over into the Afghans' orchards knowing that they'd shoot at us. We asked our parents to send citric acid in their letters so that we could dissolve it in water and drink it. It was so sour that it burned your stomach.

Before our first battle they played the Soviet national anthem. The deputy political commander gave us a talk. I remember he said we'd only beaten the Americans here by one hour, and everybody was waiting to welcome us back home as heroes.

I had no idea how to kill. Before the army I was a racing cyclist. I'd never so much as seen a real knife fight, and here I was, driving along on the back of an armoured personnel carrier. I hadn't felt like this before: powerful, strong and secure. The hills suddenly looked low, the irrigation ditches small, the trees few and far between. After half an hour I was so relaxed I felt like a tourist, taking a look at a foreign country.

We drove over a ditch on a little clay bridge: I remember being amazed it could take the weight of several tons of metal. Suddenly there was an explosion and the APC in front had got a direct hit from a grenade launcher. Men I knew were already being carried away, like stuffed animals with their arms dangling. I couldn't make sense of this new, frightening world. We sent all our mortars into where the firing had come from, several mortars to every homestead. After the battle we scraped our own guys off the armour plate with spoons. There weren't any identification discs for fatalities; I suppose they thought they might fall into the wrong hands. It was like in the song: *We don't live in a house on a street, Our address is the USSR.* So we just spread a tarpaulin over the bodies, a 'communal grave'. War hadn't even been declared; we were fighting a war that did not exist.

A Mother

I sat by Sasha's coffin saying, 'Who is it? Is that you, son?' I just kept repeating over and over, 'Is that you?' They decided I was out of my mind. Later on, I wanted to know how my son had died. I went to the Military Commissariat and the commissar started shouting at me, telling me it was a state secret that my son had died, that I shouldn't run around telling everyone.

My son was in the Vitebsk parachute division. When I went to see him take his oath of allegiance, I didn't recognize him; he stood so tall.

'Hey, how come I've got such a small mum?'

'Because I miss you and I've stopped growing.'

He bent down and kissed me, and somebody took a photograph. It's the only photograph of him as a soldier that I've got.

After the oath he had a few hours free time. We went to the park and sat down on the grass. He took his boots off because his feet were all blistered and bleeding. The previous day his unit had been on a fifty kilometre forced march and there hadn't been any size forty-six boots, so they had given him forty-fours.

'We had to run with rucksacks filled with sand. What do you reckon? Where did I come?'

'Last, probably, with those boots.'

'Wrong, mum. I was first. I took the boots off and ran. And I didn't tip sand out like some of the others.'

That night, they let the parents sleep inside the unit on mats laid out in the sports hall, but we didn't lie down until far into the night, instead we wandered round the barracks where our sons were asleep. I hoped I would get to see him when they went to do their morning gymnastics but they were all running in identical striped vests and I missed him, didn't catch a last glimpse of him. They all went to the toilet in a line, in a line to do their gymnastics, in a line to the canteen. They didn't let them do anything on their own because, when the boys had heard they were being sent to Afghanistan, one hanged himself in the toilet and two others slashed their wrists. They were under guard.

His second letter began, 'Greetings from Kabul . . . ' I screamed so loudly that the neighbours ran in. It was the first time since Sasha was born that I was sorry I had not got married and had no one to look after me.

Sasha used to tease me. 'Why don't you get married, Mum?'

'Because you'd be jealous.'

He'd laugh and say nothing. We were going to live together for a long, long time to come.

I got a few more letters and then there was silence, such a long silence I wrote to the commander of his unit. Straight away Sasha wrote back to me, 'Mum, please don't write to the commander again. I couldn't write to you. I got my hand stung by a wasp. I didn't want to ask someone else to write, because you'd have been worried by the different handwriting.' I knew immediately that he had been wounded, and now if even a day went by without a letter from him my legs would give way under me. One of his letters was very cheerful. 'Hurray, hurray! We escorted a column back to the Union. We went with them as far as the frontier. They wouldn't let us go any further, but at least we got a distant look at our homeland. It's the best country in the world.' In his last letter he wrote, 'If I last the summer, I'll be back.'

On 29 August I decided summer was over. I bought Sasha a new suit and a pair of shoes, which are still in the wardrobe now. The next day, before I went to work I took off my ear-rings and my ring. For some reason I couldn't bear to wear them. That was the day on which he was killed.

When they brought the zinc coffin into the room, I lay on top of it and measured it again and again. One metre, two metres. He was two metres tall. I measured with my hands to make sure the coffin was the right size for him. The coffin was sealed, so I couldn't kiss him one last time, or touch him, I didn't even know what he was wearing, I just talked to the coffin like a madwoman.

I said I wanted to choose the place in the cemetery for him myself. They gave me two injections, and I went there with my brother. There were 'Afghan' graves on the main avenue.

'Lay my son here too. He'll be happier among his friends.'

I can't remember who was there with us. Some official. He shook his head. 'We are not permitted to bury them together. They have to be dispersed throughout the cemetery.'

They say there was a case where they brought a coffin back to a mother, and she buried it, and a year later her son came back alive. He'd only been wounded. I never saw my son's body, or kissed him goodbye. I'm still waiting.

A Nurse

Every day I was there I told myself I was a fool to come. Especially at night, when I had no work to do. All I thought during the day was 'How can I help them all?' I couldn't believe anybody would make the bullets they were using. Whose idea were they? The point of entry was small, but inside, their intestines, their liver, their spleen were all ripped and torn apart. As if it wasn't enough to kill or wound them, they had to be put through that kind of agony as well. They always cried for their mothers when they were in pain, or frightened. I never heard them call for anyone else.

They told us it was a just war. We were helping the Afghan people to put an end to feudalism and build a socialist society. Somehow they didn't get round to mentioning that our men were being killed. For the whole of the first month I was there they just dumped the amputated arms and legs of our soldiers and officers, even their bodies, right next to the tents. It was something I would hardly have believed if I had seen it in films about the Civil War. There were no zinc coffins then: they hadn't got round to manufacturing them.

Twice a week we had political indoctrination. They went on about our sacred duty, and how the border must be inviolable. Our superior ordered us to inform on every wounded soldier, every patient. It was called monitoring the state of morale: the army must be healthy! We weren't to feel compassion. But we did feel compassion: it was the only thing that held everything together.

A Regimental Press Officer

I will begin at the point where everything fell apart.

We were advancing on Jalalabad and a little girl of about seven years old was standing by the roadside. Her arm had been smashed and was held on only by a thread, as if she were a torn rag doll. She had dark eyes like olives, and they were fixed on me. I jumped down from the vehicle to take her in my arms and carry her to our nurses, but she sprang back terrified and screaming like a small animal. Still screaming she ran away, her little arm dangling and looking as though it would come off completely. I ran after her shouting, caught up with her and pressed her to me, stroking her. She was biting and scratching, trembling all over, as if some wild animal had seized her. It was only then that the thought struck me like a thunderbolt: she didn't believe I wanted to help her; she thought I wanted to kill her. The way she ran away, the way she shuddered, how afraid she was of me are things I'll never forget.

I had set out for Afghanistan with idealism blazing in my eyes. I had been told that the Afghans needed me, and I believed it. While I was there I never dreamed about the war, but now every night I am back running after that little girl with her olive eyes, and her little arm dangling as if it's going to fall off any moment.

Out there you felt quite differently about your country. 'The Union', we called it. It seemed there was something great and powerful behind us, something which would always stand up for us. I remember, though, the evening after one battle—there had been losses, men killed and men seriously injured—we plugged in the television to forget about it, to see what was going on in the Union. A mammoth new factory had been built in Siberia; the Queen of England had given a banquet in honour of some VIP; youths in Voronezh had raped two schoolgirls for the hell of it; a prince had been killed in Africa. The country was going about its business and we felt completely useless. Someone had to turn the television off, before we shot it to pieces.

It was a mothers' war. They were in the thick of it. The people at large didn't suffer, they didn't know what was going on. They were told we were fighting bandits. In nine years a regular army of 100,000 troops couldn't beat some ragged bandits? An army with the latest technology. (God help anyone who got in the way of an artillery bombardment with our Hail or Hurricane rocket launchers: the telegraph poles flew like matchsticks.) The 'bandits' had only old Maxim machine-guns we had seen in films, the Stingers and Japanese machine guns came later. We'd bring in prisoners, emaciated people with big, peasant hands. They were no bandits. They were the people of Afghanistan.

The war had its own ghastly rules: if you were photographed or if you shaved before a battle, you were dead. It was always the blue-eyed heroes who were the first to be killed: you'd meet one of those types and before you knew it, he was dead. People mostly got killed either in their first months when they were too curious, or towards the end when they'd lost their sense of caution and become stupid. At night you'd forget where you were, who you were, what you were doing there. No one could sleep during the last six or eight weeks before they went home.

Here in the Union we are like brothers. A young guy going down the street on crutches with a shiny medal can only be one of us. You might only sit down on a bench and smoke a cigarette together, but you feel as if you've been talking to each other the whole day.

The authorities want to use us to clamp down on organized crime. If there is any trouble to be broken up, the police send for 'the Afghans'. As far as they are concerned we are guys with big fists and small brains who nobody likes. But surely if your hand

hurts you don't put it in the fire, you look after it until it gets
better.

A Mother

I skip along to the cemetery as if I'm on my way to meet
someone. I feel I'm going to visit my son. Those first days I stayed
there all night. It wasn't frightening. I'm waiting for the spring,
for a little flower to burst through to me out of the ground. I
planted snowdrops, so I would have a greeting from my son as
early as possible. They come to me from down there, from him.

I'll sit with him until evening and far on into the night.
Sometimes I don't realize I've started wailing until I scare the
birds, a whole squall of crows, circling and flapping above me
until I come to my senses and stop. I've gone there every day for
four years, in the evening if not in the morning. I missed eleven
days when I was in hospital, then I ran away in the hospital gown
to see my son.

He called me 'Mother mine', and 'Angel mother mine'.
'Well, angel mother mine, your son has been accepted
by the Smolensk Military Academy. I trust you are pleased.'
He sat down at the piano and sang.

Gentlemen officers, princes indeed!
If I'm not first among them,
I'm one of their breed.

My father was a regular officer who died in the defence of
Leningrad. My grandfather was an officer too. My son was made
to be a military man—he had the bearing, so tall and strong. He
should have been a hussar with white gloves, playing cards.

Everybody wanted to be like him. Even I, his own mother,
would imitate him. I would sit down at the piano the way he did,
and sometimes start walking the way he did, especially after he
was killed. I so much want him always to be present in me.

W hen he first went to Afghanistan, he didn't write for ages. I waited and waited for him to come home on leave. Then one day the telephone rang at work.

'Angel mother mine, I am home.'

I went to meet him off the bus. His hair had gone grey. He didn't admit he wasn't on leave, that he'd asked to be let out of hospital for a couple of days to see his mother. He'd got hepatitis, malaria and everything else rolled into one but he warned his sister not to tell me. I went into his room again before I went off to work, to see him sleeping. He opened his eyes. I asked him why he was not asleep, it was so early. He said he'd had a bad dream.

We went with him as far as Moscow. It was lovely, sunny May weather, and the trees were in bloom. I asked him what it was like over there.

'Mother mine, Afghanistan is something we have no business to be doing.' He looked only at me, not at anyone else. 'I don't want to go back into that hole. I really do not.' He walked away, but turned round, 'It's as simple as that, Mum.' He never said 'Mum'. The woman at the airport desk was in tears watching us.

When I woke up on 7 July I hadn't been crying. I stared glassily at the ceiling. He had woken me, as if he had come to say goodbye. It was eight o'clock. I had to get ready to go to work. I was wandering with my dress from the bathroom to the sitting-room, from one room to another. For some reason I couldn't bear to put that light-coloured dress on. I felt dizzy, and couldn't see people properly. Everything was blurred. I grew calmer towards lunch-time, towards midday.

The seventh day of July. He had seven cigarettes in his pocket, seven matches. He had taken seven pictures with his camera. He had written seven letters to me, and seven to his girlfriend. The book on his bedside table was open at page seven. It was Kobo Abe's *Containers of Death*.

He had three or four seconds in which he could have saved himself. They were hurtling over a precipice in a vehicle. He couldn't be the first to jump out. He never could.

From Deputy Regimental Commander for Political Affairs, Major S. R. Sinelnikov. In fulfilment of my duty as a soldier, I have to inform you that Senior Lieutenant Valerii Gennadievich Volovich was killed today at 1045 hours.

The whole city already knew all about it. In the Officers' Club they'd put up black crêpe and his photograph. The plane bringing his coffin was due at any minute, but nobody had told me a thing. They couldn't bring themselves to speak. At work everybody's faces were tear-stained. I asked, 'What has happened?'

They tried to distract me in various ways. A friend came round, then finally a doctor in a white coat arrived. I told him he was crazy, that boys like my son did not get killed. I started hammering the table. I ran over to the window and started beating the glass. They gave me an injection. I kept on shouting. They gave me another injection, but that had no effect, either; I was screaming, 'I want to see him, take me to my son.' Eventually they had to take me.

There was a long coffin. The wood was unplaned, and written on it in large letters in yellow paint was 'Volovich'. I had to find him a place in the cemetery, somewhere dry, somewhere nice and dry. If that meant a fifty rouble bribe, fine. Here, take it, only make sure it's a good place, nice and dry. Inside I knew how disgusting that was, but I just wanted a nice dry place for him. Those first nights I didn't leave him. I stayed there. They would take me off home, but I would come back.

When I go to see him I bow, and when I leave I bow again. I never get cold even in freezing temperatures; I write my letters there; I am only ever at home when I have visitors. When I walk back to my house at night the streetlamps are lit, the cars have their headlamps on. I feel so strong that I am not afraid of anything.

Only now am I waking from my sorrow which is like waking from sleep. I want to know whose fault this was. Why doesn't anybody say anything? Why aren't we being told who did it? Why aren't they being put on trial?

I greet every flower on his grave, every little root and stem. 'Have you come from there? Do you come from him? You have come from my son.

Translated from the Russian by Arch Tait.

Timothy Garton Ash
We The People

We The People is the eye-witness account, by one of Europe's most
informed political observers, of one of Europe's most important political
moments. As one communist regime fell after another in 1989, Timothy
Garton Ash was there to witness the collapse.

He was in Warsaw when the government was humiliated by
Solidarity in the elections. He was in Budapest when Imre Nagy was
finally given his proper burial. He was in Berlin as the Wall opened.
And he was in Prague with Václav Havel and the members of Civic
Forum, as they made their 'Velvet Revolution'.

'It is with minimal exaggeration that I state that, in the future, there
will probably be streets in Warsaw, Prague and Budapest bearing the
name of Timothy Garton Ash.'
Karel Kyncl, *Independent*

Paperback £4.99 ISBN 0140 14023-9
Also available in paperback from Granta Books by
Timothy Garton Ash: *The Uses of Adversity, Essays on the Fate of Central
Europe*, winner of the 1989 European Essay Prize.

PEREGRINE HODSON
WAR MEMORIES

Tokyo: I had lunch with a friend of a friend, Harry Sasaki. He is a well-preserved man in his late sixties, with an erect posture, silvery hair and a gentle manner. I wouldn't have guessed he was a war criminal.

Christina told me he was the most unlikely war criminal she knew, and I laughed. When I met him I knew what she meant. He spoke with a perfect American accent. He wore a dark brown tweed jacket, dark grey trousers, a thick cotton shirt and a wool tie. We sat down for lunch in a room at the top of the Imperial Hotel, overlooking the Imperial Palace, and he ordered a couple of beers and asked after Christina. He said he was looking forward to seeing her when she was next in Tokyo. I could see that he wondered how much Christina had told me about him.

'I hear you were a convicted war criminal' didn't sound right. 'Would you like to talk about some of your war experiences in the Philippines?' didn't sound much better. I wasn't sure what to say. War crimes aren't the easiest topic of conversation with a convicted war criminal. Not five minutes into a first meeting.

I explained that I was in Japan on business, and he relaxed a bit. I asked him how he had acquired such good American pronunciation. He smiled and began his story. His father had a small silk business in Niigata in the late 1920s. When the silk market collapsed, he decided to sell up and take his wife and two sons to a new life in America. Harry was eight years old and his younger brother was three.

'In every way it was a whole new world for me,' he said. After the mountains of Niigata he found California to be big and strange and exciting. The people were friendly and Harry was soon speaking English at school, although at home his parents spoke Japanese. His father worked in a canning factory. His mother stayed and continued her previous way of life: she cooked Japanese food, made Japanese pickles and kept the old festivals. The boys were expected to observe the traditions of their homeland.

By the time Harry went to high school he was bilingual in English and Japanese. After graduating he decided to visit Japan and took a ship to Yokohama. It was 1939. He returned to the village where he was born. 'I was coming home.' Harry smiled, then frowned. 'It started so beautiful and ended so ugly.' Like snow, I thought, but I didn't say anything. I wasn't sure if he was talking about the war or Japan or himself.

I said I thought it was difficult to judge the actions of war in peace because war and peace are different worlds. He suddenly looked very old and tired and said that he lived with the memory of the war every day. It wasn't exactly a confession but I thought I understood what he was saying. 'It's not possible to judge the past,' he said, 'but people remember.' I was about to ask him which people when, as if he heard what I was thinking, he said, 'I remember.'

A few months before, he was in a bookshop and saw a book about the war in the Philippines written by his commanding officer. He read a few pages and realized it was all lies. As he told me this his expression reminded me of the face of a demon guardian at the gate of a temple. 'Whatever happened during the war, it's wrong to lie about the past,' he said. 'It's shameful.' We agreed that people who forget the mistakes of the past are condemned to repeat them. The waiter came and asked if we wanted sandwiches.

While we waited for our order to arrive, Harry told me about his time in prison. The food was better than anything he'd had during the war—sometimes there was so much he couldn't eat all of it. Meanwhile, outside the prison, people in Japan were starving. He got on well with the American guards and was put in charge of the prison library. He decided to read the Bible. When he was growing up in the States the only English books he read were the ones his teachers told him to read: facts and figures. If he read for pleasure, he read Japanese books which his father recommended. I asked him why he chose to read the Bible and he smiled. 'Because I was feeling bad and I remembered people in the States calling it "the good book". Reading it didn't make me feel any better, but it helped me understand a lot of things about the Americans and the British.'

After he finished the Bible he made a reading plan for the thirty years of his sentence. He kept to it methodically and read his way through the complete works of Shakespeare and Dickens and several other authors, before he was released, his sentence shortened to ten years. I thought of him sitting in his cell, making his way through *Dombey and Son* and *The Pickwick Papers*.

Did it occur to him that he might have been a traitor to America? Did he search in desperation for some way to return to life as it was before everything went wrong? Had he simply adopted the taboos, shibboleths and customs of the conquerors? I wanted to ask him, but the sandwiches arrived and instead we talked more about food, about Kobe beef, Texas beef and clam chowder.

I looked for a sign, something in his eyes or face which might explain why he was tried and found guilty of war crimes. I saw nothing. He didn't defend the past; he didn't deny it; he seemed to accept it. If he felt guilt he showed no sign of it. He had spent time in prison and had been released. He had paid his dues and he was a free man.

He told me that he worries about his wife who suffers from arthritis and that he's proud of his son who works for one of the big securities companies. He enjoys his work in the travel business and likes going to the United States. 'It's a great place to visit,' he joked, 'but I wouldn't want to live there.' We finished our meal and Harry insisted on paying. As we shook hands and said goodbye to each other in the hotel lobby, Harry said he hoped we'd meet again. 'Any friend of Christina's is a friend of mine.'

I thanked him and said I hoped we'd meet soon. He turned to walk away. I glanced behind me at an electronic map of the world, covering the wall of the lobby, that showed the different times in the major cities. It was two o'clock in the afternoon in Tokyo, six in the morning in London and ten the night before in Los Angeles. I turned back and looked for Harry Sasaki. There were several men like him in the lobby, wearing raincoats, with silvery hair. But no Harry.

2

The following Friday I saw Harry again. We arranged to meet outside the station at Shibuya, by the statue of Sachiko, at one o'clock. The sun was shining and the crowds outside the station were dressed in summer colours. I joined a group of people standing by the statue. I carried a newspaper but I didn't read it.

It was almost one and I began to worry that Harry might not come. I was nervous. Our last meeting went well: there was an understanding between us. But perhaps I had imagined it. It was hard to see why an old man should travel across Tokyo to meet someone he hardly knew, to talk about things most people would be happy to forget.

Then I saw him. I was surprised at how old and frail he was. He was wearing a light grey suit and was using a bamboo walking-stick. We shook hands. The shape of his hand in mine was like an old friend's.

We had lunch in the Seibu department store. There was a lot of background noise and Harry's voice wasn't loud enough for the micro-cassette, so I took notes. Harry asked if I'd heard from Christina. I told him that she sent her love and hoped to see him soon. He smiled and I thought, what a nice grandfather he would be. I knew he was waiting for me to ask questions, but it didn't feel right to begin, so I said something about the weather and he said it would soon be the rainy season. He told me how important the seasons are to the Japanese.

'We Japanese are deeply affected by the seasons. Every haiku has its season-word. Scroll paintings in a tea room are changed according to the season, with cherry blossoms in spring and chrysanthemums in autumn.' He asked if he was talking too fast for me. I thanked him and said no, I understood what he was saying; but wasn't the Japanese attitude to the passing of time Buddhist? I had thought that the cycles of death and rebirth, the wheel of the law and the wheel of suffering, led finally to Buddha, to the great enlightenment.

Harry said yes, but Japan's religion is Shinto. The week before he had read in a newspaper a survey of Japan's religious beliefs: seventy-five per cent of Japanese described themselves as Buddhists, ninety-five per cent as Shinto. 'The survey wasn't wrong,' he said. 'It showed the way we think of ourselves. We're Shinto when we go to the shrine for a festival, or when someone is born or gets married; we're Buddhist when someone dies or when we think about the past and the future life.'

I asked him whether he thought of himself as a Buddhist or a Shinto.

'When I think about it, I'm Buddhist. But I feel Shinto.' He looked at me through his gold-rimmed spectacles with an expression that was melancholy and comical, and asked if I understood. I said I did. As I listened to him I was thinking that I had intended to ask him about the war, and that instead we were talking about the weather, the seasons, Shinto and how the Japanese love nature. There was something artificial in the conversation but the *kimochi*—the feeling—was good between us. I felt it was a good moment to begin asking questions. I asked what it was like in Japan just before the Second World War. Was there an atmosphere of idealism and pride? Was the war a great adventure? Harry thought for a moment.

'I was carried by the current and dragged along. I was still young, you know.' He cleared his throat. 'You learn a lot later. That's what happened to me. I learned a lot later, after the country was defeated. I wasn't particularly conscious of the military. I didn't want to fight. I didn't want to kill anyone.'

Had he ever considered that what was happening was wrong? 'I couldn't say it openly, because of my weakness. In those circumstances you have to follow—.' I could see he was having difficulty finding the right word. He clicked his fingers softly, as if to call the word from the air. 'You have to follow the—you know.'

He told me he was a liaison officer with the local population in the Philippines. 'I tried to call people from the hiding places, to call them back to their villages. I was happy to help the people. I had to go to the countryside. There were people hiding out there, maybe for a year or so. This work went on for a while, maybe until Christmas 1941. Then we moved to Manila. I was a civilian, but I was doing liaison work there between the Japanese army and the people. It was a sort of public relations job.' I interrupted him to ask if he was in the intelligence service and he said yes, he was.

'MacArthur came back, the situation went the other way and the HQ had to move north. The Japanese army rounded up so-called guerrillas and the people. They started to kill guerrillas and villagers, and the case of the war crime took place.' I asked what the charge was at his trial.

'I was part of, you know, the planning and the execution of the plot. Yes.' He paused. 'They rounded up Chinese and Filipinos and executed them. Not only in my town, but other places. There were many kinds of excuses given by garrison commanders. Finally it happened in my town.' He repeated the phrase 'the planning and execution of the plot.' I could imagine the same words, the same sentence, repeated during his trial.

'The planning and execution of the plot'—he paused—'the incineration of the town. In fact it was partly done by the Japanese garrison, and partly by American bombing.' For a moment I forgot which war we were talking about. The words 'American bombing' made me think of Vietnam. I was only half-listening to what Harry was saying. I looked at what I'd written: 'Massacring . . .' The sentence was unfinished. I asked if there was anything he could have done to prevent the massacre.

He took a deep breath. 'I did my best to ensure it wouldn't take place. I couldn't do much, you see. I was at one meeting where a plan for the massacre was being discussed, and a senior officer was against the plan and I agreed that it shouldn't be done. And that was when my opinion was expressed. I wasn't an officer or a soldier. I was just a civilian attached to the army.'

'What happened?' I asked.

'My view was not very effective. The commander forced the garrison to carry out the action. Six hundred Chinese were killed in a coconut grove. And sixty Filipinos.' Harry was silent. I felt I had to say something, so I asked how they had died.

'I don't think by shooting. Mostly by bayonet and by beheading with the Japanese sword—the *katana*.' He frowned and shook his head. 'But to kill six hundred people—no officer could use a sword on so many. I guess the soldiers used their bayonets.' I studied his face. He was telling me about a coconut grove in the Philippines fifty years ago, and we were sitting in a Tokyo restaurant full of men in business suits and waitresses in smart orange and white uniforms. I thought of the blindfolds, if they were used, and the heat, and the sound of insects. I looked at the men in suits at the table next to us who were eating Pacific prawns, and at Harry Sasaki, who was breaking a bread roll. His fingers trembled, and he succeeded in breaking the bread only after repeated efforts. He looked up from his plate.

'War can make people crazy,' he said. 'You can't tell what's going to happen. You can't imagine how it is when your comrades die. I saw several die. They didn't shout "*Banzai!*" or "Long Live the Emperor!" They used to say "*oka-san, oka-san*"—"Mother, mother." '

'I had a friend, a special friend,' he sighed, 'The Filipino guerrillas knew he was a good man but they had to kill him.'

I asked why. Harry laughed.

'Because he was Japanese. Everyone hated the Japanese at that time. Nobody picked him up. Nobody tried to help him. He died, and his body was left to rot. I tried to find his grave. Four years ago I went back with his three sons to try to find his grave. There was nothing there. I asked some ex-guerrillas about what happened to him. They showed me the place where he died, and told me how his head was this way and his legs were that way, but there was nothing there. Dogs must have taken all the bones away.' Harry shook his head. 'The young people from that time are old now. What we've gone through! Now people are repeating the same thing. Nothing's been learned.

'I tried to fight against evil.' Harry laughed an old man's laugh: dry, resigned to the past. 'I tried to fight against evil and—.' I waited for him to finish the sentence. He looked at me through his spectacles. 'Sometimes you can't win over the evil,' he said. 'The evil took place. Despite my intentions, I was involved in evil and sentenced to thirty years hard labour.' The way he presented the crime and punishment, in one sentence, joined together by the word 'and', was like an accusation, confession and statement of belief, all in one. I asked if he could have acted otherwise than he had. He considered for a moment and said, 'Well, I don't know what I could have done.'

A waitress arrived and placed our orders on the table. Harry drank some water. I waited until the waitress had finished arranging the dishes before asking Harry if he thought he had had a fair trial.

'My trial—it wasn't fair at all. But some kind of trial had to
be conducted. It was necessary. Being objective was difficult at
the trial, and it's difficult now. The prosecutor and the judge
tried to investigate everything but they were human beings.' I
wasn't sure what he was saying.

'At the time of the trial no Filipinos could speak in favour of
Japan.' He paused and I thought he had finished. But then he
continued: 'As I told you, I was between the Japanese army and
the people. I was like a middle-man. On the day of the incident,
all the men, the Filipino men, were rounded up and assembled in
the church to be taken away. I was there. It was my job to tell
each man that he had to stay or could go. I was a liaison officer,
so I'd got to know a lot of people, including a lady from a group
of young Filipinas doing charity work. This lady used to contact
me for rice and other provisions, and that's how she helped the
poor people.' Harry hesitated. 'We knew each other. At the time
of the incident, when the people were gathered in the church to
be taken away, the lady came to me with her girlfriend and asked
me to save her brother. That's what I did. I saved him.

'She was called as a witness at my trial. The prosecutor
asked her if I was guilty of the crime. She said yes, that man
should be executed. The prosecutor asked her why and she said,
"Because he is Japanese." ' Harry looked down at the table, as if
he was looking over a distant landscape, and I wondered about
the relationship between the young Japanese liaison officer and
young Filipina lady who did charity work for poor people. Harry
cleared his throat.

'When I was in prison I wrote to her. I asked her why she
said such things at the trial. I thought that perhaps she was
forced to by the prosecutor. But she never answered. It's difficult
to be objective. It's the kind of contradiction that's hard to get
out of.' Suddenly he was an old man talking about things that
happened a long time ago. I asked if he was tired but he said he
felt fine.

He returned to the trial. 'The judge read the facts, the story,
the written facts, and made his decision and passed sentence on
everyone involved. The court was influenced by the politicians;
the witnesses were influenced by their fear of being tried as

collaborators. It's normal. Everyone is a victim of circumstances. I was carried by the current. I guess it was the same with the lady. But what made her say, "Because he is Japanese?" '

AMITAV GHOSH
AN EGYPTIAN IN BAGHDAD

The last time I spoke to Nabeel was over a year ago. He was in Baghdad. I was in New York. It wasn't easy getting through. The directory listed a code for Baghdad, but after days of trying, all I'd got was a recorded message telling me that the number I'd dialled didn't exist.

In the end I had to book a call with the operator. She took a while, but eventually there was a voice at the other end, speaking in the blunt, rounded Arabic of Iraq: 'Yes? Who is it?'

Nabeel's family had told me that he was working as an assistant in a photographer's shop. The owner was an Iraqi and Nabeel had been working for him since 1986, when he left his village in Egypt and went to Iraq. There was a telephone in the shop and the owner was relatively kind, a relatively kind Iraqi, and he allowed Nabeel to receive calls.

I imagined him as a big, paunchy man, Nabeel's boss, sitting at the end of a counter, behind a cash box, with the telephone beside him and a Kodacolor poster of a snow-clad mountain on the wall above. He was wearing a blue *gallabeyya* and a white lace cap; he had a carefully trimmed moustache and a pair of sun-glasses in his breast pocket. The telephone beside him was of the old-fashioned kind, black and heavy, and it had a brass lock fastened in its dial. The boss kept the key, and Nabeel and the other assistants had to ask for it when they wanted to make a call. It was late at night in New York, so it had to be morning in Baghdad. The shop must just have opened. They had probably had no customers yet.

'Is Nabeel there?' I asked.

'Who?' said the voice.

'Nabeel Idris Badawy,' I said. 'The Egyptian.'

He grunted. '*Wa min inta?*' he said. 'And who're you?'

'I'm a friend of his,' I said. 'Tell him it's his friend from India. He'll know.'

'What's that?' he said. 'From where?'

'From India, *ya raiyis*,' I said. 'Could you tell him? And quickly if you please, for I'm calling from America.'

'From America?' he shouted down the line. 'But you said you're Indian?'

'Yes, I am—I'm just in America on a visit. Nabeel quickly, if you please, *ya raiyis . . .*'

I heard him shout across the room: '*Ya* Nabeel, somebody wants to talk to you, some Indian or something . . .'

I could tell from Nabeel's first words of greeting that my call had taken him completely by surprise. It was only natural. Eight years had passed since I'd left his village. He and his family had befriended me when I was living there in 1980 and 1981, doing research. I was then in my mid-twenties; Nabeel was a few years younger. We had become close friends, and for the first few years after I'd left, we had written letters back and forth, between India and Egypt. But then he had gone to do his National Service, in the army, and he'd stopped writing. In time I had stopped writing too. He had no way of knowing that I would be in the US on a visit that year. Until a few weeks ago I hadn't known that he was in Baghdad. I knew now because I had just been to Egypt and had visited his village and his family.

'Nabeel's not here *ya* Amitab,' his sister-in-law, Fawzia, had said to me, once she recovered from the shock of seeing me at the door. 'He's not in the village—he's gone to Iraq.'

Ushering me in she fussed about distractedly, pumping her kerosene stove, fetching tea and sugar. She was a pretty, good-humoured woman who had always made me welcome in their house. I had been in the village when she was married to Nabeel's elder brother Aly.

'Nabeel left about two years ago,' she said. 'He went with his cousin Ismail, do you remember him?'

I did. He was Nabeel's best friend as well as his cousin, although they could not have been more different. Ismail was lively, energetic, always ready with a joke or a pun; Nabeel, on the other hand, was thoughtful and serious, with a marked disinclination for vigorous activity of any kind. When he made his way down the lanes of the village it was in a stately, considered kind of way, in marked contrast to the caperings of his cousin.

'They left for Iraq soon after they finished their National Service,' said Fawzia. 'They went to make money.'

They had rented a room in Baghdad with some other young

175

men from the village, she said, and they all lived and cooked and ate together. She had taught Nabeel and Ismail to cook a few things before they left, so they managed all right. Ismail was a construction labourer. There was good money to be had in construction; Nabeel earned less as a photographer's assistant, but he liked his job. Ismail had been trying to get him to go into construction, but Nabeel wasn't interested.

'You know him,' she said, laughing. 'He always wanted a job where he wouldn't have to get his clothes dirty.'

Later, when her husband Aly had come home from the fields, and we had all had dinner, she gave me the number of the shop in Baghdad. Once every couple of months or so she and Nabeel's brothers would make a trip to a post office in a nearby town and telephone him in Baghdad.

'It costs a lot,' she said, 'but you can hear him like he was in the next house.'

Nabeel couldn't telephone them of course, but now and again he would speak into a cassette recorder and send them a tape. He and his brothers had all been through high school; Nabeel himself even had a college degree. But they still found the spoken word more reassuring than the written.

'You must hear his voice on the machine,' said Aly and produced a tape. He placed it carefully inside a huge cassette-recorder-cum-radio and we gathered around to listen. Nabeel's voice was very solemn, and he was speaking like a Cairene, almost as though he'd forgotten the village dialect.

'Does he always talk like that now?' I asked Fawzia.

'Oh no,' she laughed. 'He's talking like that because it's a cassette. On the telephone he sounds just like he used to.'

Nabeel said almost nothing about himself and his life in Iraq; just that he was well, and that his salary had gone up. He listed in detail the names of all the people he wanted them to convey his greetings to—members of his lineage, people in the village, his school friends. Then he told them about everyone from the village who was in Iraq—that so-and-so was well, that someone had moved to another city and that someone else was about to go home. For the rest he gave his family precise instructions about what they were to do with the money he was sending them; about the additions they were to make to the house, exactly how the rooms should look, how much they should spend on the floors, the windows, the roof. His brothers listened, rapt, although they must have heard the tape through several times already.

Later, Aly wrote down Nabeel's address for me. It consisted of a number on a numbered street in 'New Baghdad'. I pictured to myself an urban development project of the kind that flourishes in the arid hinterlands of Cairo and New Delhi—straight, treeless streets and blocks of yellow buildings divided into 'Pockets', 'Phases' and 'Zones'.

'You must telephone him,' one of Nabeel's younger brothers said. 'He'll be so pleased. Do you know, he's kept all your letters, wrapped in a plastic bag? He still talks of you, a lot. Tell me, didn't you once say to him . . .'

And then he recounted, almost word-for-word, a conversation I had once had with Nabeel. It was about something trivial, about my college in Delhi, but for some reason I had written it down in my diary, that very day, while it was still fresh in my memory. I had read through my diaries of that time again, recently. That was why I knew that Nabeel's brother had repeated that conversation, or at least a part of it, almost verbatim, in near exact detail. I was amazed. It seemed to me an impossible, deeply moving defiance of time and the laws of hearsay and memory.

'You can be sure that I will telephone him,' I said to Nabeel's brother. 'I'll telephone him soon, from America.'

'You must tell him that we are well and that he should send another cassette.'

'Won't he be surprised,' said Fawzia, 'when he hears Amitab's voice on the phone? He'll think someone's playing a joke on him.'

'We'll write and tell him,' said Aly. 'We'll write tomorrow so he won't be surprised. We'll tell him that you're going to phone him from America.'

But they hadn't written: the surprise in Nabeel's voice as he greeted me over the phone was proof of that. And I, for my part, even though I had the advantage, was almost as amazed as Nabeel, though for a different reason. When I was living in their village, in 1980 and '81, Nabeel and Ismail had had very definite plans for their immediate future: they wanted salaried jobs in the Agriculture Ministry. It would not have occurred to any of us then to think that within a few years they would both be abroad and that I would be able to speak to them on the phone from thousands of miles away.

There was only one telephone in the village then. It had never worked as far as anyone knew. It was not meant to—it was really a badge of office, a sceptre. It belonged to the government, and it resided in the house of the village headman. When a headman was voted out in the local elections, the telephone was ritually removed from his house and taken to the victor's. It was carried at the head of a procession, accompanied by drums and gunshots, as though it were a saint's relics. 'We carried the telephone that year,' people would say, meaning 'we swept the elections'.

Nabeel's family was one of the poorest in the village—and the village was not by any means prosperous. Few families in the village had more than five *feddans* of land, but most had one or two. Nabeel's family had none at all. That was one of the reasons why he and his brothers had all got an education: schools and colleges were free, and they had no land to claim their time.

Nabeel lived with his parents in a three-room adobe hut, along with Aly and Fawzia and their three other brothers. Aly worked in the fields, for a daily wage, when there was work to be had; their father earned a tiny salary as a village watchman. He was a small, frail man with sunken cheeks and watery grey eyes. As a watchman he had the possession of a gun, an ancient Enfield, that was kept in a locked chest under his bed. He said that he'd last had occasion to use it some fifteen years ago when somebody spotted a gang of thieves running through Hassan Bassiuni's cornfields. The thieves had escaped but the gun had mowed down half the field—it was really very much like a blunderbuss. He was very proud of it. Once when a fire broke out in Shahata Hammoudah's house and everyone was busy doing what they could, I noticed Nabeel's father running in the opposite direction. When I next looked around he was standing at attention in front of the burning house, holding his gun, smiling benignly.

Nabeel's mother, a dark, fine-boned woman, secretly despaired of her husband. 'He's been defeated by the world,' she would say sometimes, 'There's no one to stand beside Nabeel and his brothers except themselves.'

Now, eight years later, Nabeel's father and mother were both dead. 'And the saddest thing,' Fawzia said to me, 'is that they didn't live to see how things have changed for us.'

The three mud-walled rooms were gone now. In their place was a bungalow, or at least, its skeleton—four or five rooms, in a largely unfinished state, but built of brick and cement and entirely habitable. There was provision for a bathroom, a kitchen, a living-room, as well as another entire apartment upstairs, exactly like the one below. That was where Nabeel would live once he was married, Fawzia said to me. She, for her part, was content: in her house she now had a television set, a cassette recorder, and a washing-machine.

It wasn't just her life that had changed. When I first came to the village in 1980, there were only three or four television sets there, and they belonged to the handful of men who owned fifteen to twenty *feddans* of land, the richest men in the village. Those men still had their fifteen to twenty *feddans* of land and their black-and-white television sets. It was the families who had once been thought of as the poor folk of the village whose homes were now full of all the best-known brand names in Japan —television sets, washing-machines, kitchen appliances, cameras . . . I could not have begun to imagine a change on this scale when I left the village in 1981. If I had not witnessed it with my own eyes I would not have believed it possible.

It was a kind of revolution, but it had happened a long way away. It had been created entirely by the young men who had gone to work in Iraq, once that country began to experience severe labour shortages because of its war with Iran. They were carried along by a great wave of migration. In the late eighties there were estimated to be between two and three million Egyptians in Iraq. Nobody knew for sure: the wave had surged out of the country too quickly to be measured. All of Nabeel's contemporaries were gone now—all the young men with high-school educations and no jobs and no land and nothing to do but play football and lounge around the water-taps when the girls went to fetch water in the evenings. Some of the old men used to say that they would all go to the bad. But in the end it was they who had transformed the village.

'It's we who've been the real gainers in the war,' one of the village schoolteachers said to me, while I was walking down the lanes, gaping at all the newly built houses and buildings. 'The Iraqis are doing all the fighting; it's they who're dying. The Arab countries are paying them to break the back of Khomeini's Islamic revolution. For them it's a matter of survival. But in the meantime, while Iraqis are dying, others are making money. But it won't last—that money's tainted, and the price is going to be paid later, some day.'

The young men who'd left were paying a price already. 'Life is really hard there,' their families said. 'You never know what's going to happen, from day to day.' And they would tell stories about fights, about lone Egyptians being attacked on the streets, about men being forced to work inhuman hours, about how the Iraqi women would look at Egyptian men from their windows, because so many of their own men were dead, and how it always led to trouble because the Iraqis would find out and kill both the woman and the Egyptian.

'How does Nabeel like it in Iraq?' I asked his brother Aly.

'He's fine,' said Aly. 'He's all right.'

'How do you know?'

'That's what he says on the cassettes,' he said. 'I'm sure he's all right.'

'I hope so,' I said.

He was frowning now. 'God knows,' he said. 'People say life is hard out there.'

Nabeel could not tell me as much over the telephone, with his boss listening. But he was well, he said, and so was his cousin Ismail, and they were managing fine, living with their relatives and friends from back home. In turn he asked me about India, my job, my family. Then I heard a noise down the line; it sounded like another voice in the same room. Nabeel broke off to say, 'Coming, just a moment.'

I said quickly: 'I'm going back to India soon. I'll try and visit you on the way.'

'We'll be expecting you,' he said. In the background I could hear the voice again, louder now.

'You'd better go now,' I said.

'I'll tell Ismail you're coming,' he said hurriedly. 'We'll wait for you.'

But the year passed and the visit eluded me.

2

It was exactly three weeks since Saddam Hussein had invaded Kuwait, and miraculously, Abu-Ali, the old shopkeeper, was on his feet. That was how he happened to see me as I walked down the road past his window.

Nabeel's village was just a mile and a half away and I was on my way there when Abu-Ali sent a child running after me. Abu-Ali's house was where the asphalt road ended and the dirt track began. Taxi drivers would not go any further.

Now Abu-Ali was standing by the window again cradling a radio, twiddling the knob. He had always behaved as though all the village's worries had fallen on his shoulders. Now it looked as though he had taken on all of Egypt's.

The radio was a big one, with a built-in cassette recorder, but in Abu-Ali's huge, swollen hands it seemed as slim and fragile as an advanced model of calculator. It spat out a medley of electronic sounds as the pointer flashed across its face. But the sounds were lost; the noise in the room was already deafening. Abu-Ali's cousin's daughter was getting married next door. A crowd of women and children had gathered in the lane, outside their house. A boy was beating a tin wash-basin with a spoon and the women and children were clapping in time, and chanting: '*Ya rumman, ya rumman*,' singing of the bride as the bloom of a pomegranate.

At intervals Abu-Ali rose from his bed, went to the window, glared at the woman and children outside, shuffled back and collapsed on to his bed again. This was an astonishing feat. When I first knew him years ago, he was already so fat that he found it near impossible to leave his bed. Now he was fatter still. Every time he stood up his belly surged away from him, like backwash leaving a beach. It was pure greed, his neighbours had always said; he ate the way other people force-fed geese; he could eat two chickens and a pot of rice at one sitting. And now that there was all this Iraqi money in his house, that was exactly what he did sometimes—ate two whole chickens and a pot of rice, right after the midday prayers.

'Ate it,' muttered Abu-Ali, shuffling across the room yet again. 'The son of a bitch just ate it like it was a chicken's liver. Saw a tasty little morsel and just swallowed it.'

He sounded envious: an appetite was something he could understand.

'So what do you expect?' someone said. The room was quite full now; several men had stopped by to see Abu-Ali on their way to the wedding. 'What was Kuwait but a tasty little morsel cooked up by the British and sucked dry by the Americans?'

'Just ate it!' Abu-Ali twirled the knob of the radio sending the pointer screeching through a succession of stations. 'BBC, BBC,' he muttered, 'where's that son-of-a-bitch BBC?'

A distant, haranguing voice suddenly burst out of the radio, screaming shrilly. Abu-Ali started back in surprise, almost dropping the radio. 'Who's this son of a bitch now?'

'That's Damascus,' said someone.

'No it's those son-of-a-bitch Americans broadcasting in Arabic,' said someone else.

'No it's Riyadh,' said Abu-Ali. 'It sounds like a Saudi.'

'Riyadh is where he should have gone,' said another man. 'But he didn't; stopped too soon. It's those Saudi sons of bitches who should have been fixed.'

I jogged the elbow of the man sitting next to me. I knew him well once; he used to teach in a nearby school. Now he was teaching in the Yemen; he'd come home on a visit, intending to leave once the summer holidays ended. But his wife wouldn't let him go; she had four children to bring up and she was not going to let him vanish into a war zone.

'Do you know if Nabeel Badawy is back from Iraq yet?' I asked him.

'Nabeel?' he said. He'd been looking distracted, anxious, ever since he came into the room. Now he looked as though he'd been dazed by the noise and the cigarette smoke. The man next to him had his arm firmly in his grasp; he was shouting into his other ear, his voice hoarse.

'The worst sons of bitches, the most ungrateful, do you know who they are?' he shouted.

'Nabeel Idris Badawy,' I said insistently. 'You remember him?'

'The Palestinians,' shouted the man, hoarsely. 'The worst sons of bitches.'

'Nabeel Idris Badawy,' I repeated. 'From Nashawy?'

'From Nashawy?' said the schoolteacher.

'How many wars have we fought for them, you tell me? Haven't I lost my own brother?'

'Nabeel Idris Mustafa Badawy,' said the schoolteacher jubilantly, his voice rising to a shout. 'He was in Iraq; my nephew told me.'

'Them and the Israelis, God forsake them, the sons of bitches. In the end they're always at the bottom of everything.'

'I know Nabeel's in Iraq,' I shouted back. 'But do you know if he's back yet?'

He thought for a moment and then shook his head. 'No,' he said. 'I can't tell you. There are so many boys over there, you know, it's impossible to keep track. Mabrouk Hussein is still there you know, my own nephew, you remember him? And there are others from this village—there's Fahmy and Abusa and . . .'

He began to repeat the names, as everyone else who had come into the room had done. The village was a very small one, no more than 350 souls, just a hamlet really. I knew it well when I lived in the area. At that time only one man from the village was abroad; he taught Arabic in a school in Zaire. But over the last few years more than a dozen of its young men had left. Most had gone to Iraq, a couple to Jordan (it was almost the same thing). Several had returned since the beginning of the year, but five still remained, trapped in Iraq. People said their names over and over again, as though to conjure them out of Iraq, back to the village: Mabrouk, who used to keep goal; Abusa—'The Frown'—who never smiled; Fahmy, who used to ride out to the fields, on a sheep. I remembered them coming to visit me in the evenings, full of questions: 'What do you grow in India? Do you have schools? Do you have weddings? Rain? An army?' They were very young. None of them had ever been further than the local town. The machines with which they were most familiar were their *kababis*—the Persian wheels their cattle drove, round and round for hours every day, to water their fields. Mabrouk had once come running to my room, hugely excited, and dragged me away to his house to see the brand new water-pump his family had bought. It was very important for him and his family that I take a look at it, for like all the pumps in the area, it was from India (the generic name for water pump was *makana hindi*, 'the Indian machine'). No matter that I had said, time after time, that I knew nothing about water-pumps, I was always asked for an opinion when somebody bought one.

This one was exactly like the others: a big green machine with a spout, and an exhaust pipe. They had hung an old shoe on the spout and stuck an incense stick in the exhaust pipe to protect it from the evil eye. I knocked on the spout with my knuckles, and patted its diesel tank in a well-informed kind of way. 'What do you think?' Mabrouk's father said. 'Is it all right?'

I knocked a little harder, frowning.

He was anxious now: 'So, what do you think?'

I smiled: 'It's a very good one—excellent.'

There was a sigh of relief: 'Get the Indian doctor some tea.'

Mabrouk had shaken my hand: 'I knew you would be able to tell . . .'

And now Mabrouk was in the immediate vicinity of chemical

and nuclear weapons; within a few minutes' striking distance of the world's most advanced machinery. It would be he who would have to pay the price of the violence that was invented in quiet, pastoral laboratories in Heidelberg and Berkeley.

'Do you think the Americans are ever going to leave the sacred land?' a young man said at the top of his voice. People fell silent listening. Outside, the clapping seemed suddenly louder; the girls' voices more insistent.

'Never,' he shouted. 'Never—they're never going to leave the sacred places. Now that they're there, they're going to stay till the end of time. They've finally achieved what they'd never managed in a thousand years of history. And who's responsible? The Saudis—the sons of bitches.'

'*Ya rumman, ya rumman!*' the beat was growing faster, the spoons were drumming out a crescendo on the wash-basins. Glancing out of the window I saw three young men walking down the lane. They had all recently returned from Iraq; Abu-Ali's youngest son was among them. The girls stole looks at them as they walked past, singing at the tops of their voices. They were hoping perhaps that they'd stop and join in the singing and dancing, as young men used to. But these three youths walked straight past them. They had small, derisory smiles under their clipped moustaches. They were embarrassed at the sight of their sisters and cousins drumming out a beat on wash-basins while waiting for a groom who was going to arrive in a pick-up truck. They had grown accustomed to seeing weddings with big bands and hired BMWs. They were savvy, street-smart, in some ways—some of them could recite the prices of the best brand-name goods as though they'd memorized a catalogue. They could tell you what counted as a good price for anything ranging from a pair of Nike shoes to a video camera. If you'd paid a piastre more, you'd been had, someone had 'laughed at you'. The girls were going to be disappointed. These young men were not going to tie up their *gallabeyyas* and dance to the rhythm of dented wash-basins.

'Why'd you think the Americans and the British have always supported those son-of-a-bitch sheikhs?' my friend the schoolteacher said. 'Why do you think? Because it was the easiest way to get back all the money they spent on oil—it all went straight back to their casinos and hotels. And they knew some day they would be able to get back here through those sheikhs, the sons of bitches.'

The girls were beginning to irritate Abu-Ali. He shuffled up to the window and yelled: 'Will you stop that noise? Can't you see we're trying to listen to the news on the radio?'

His voice was legendary; it shook the mud floor. The girls stopped their singing, for a moment, taken by surprise. But soon they started again, softly at first, and then louder, gradually. The wedding had been planned a year ago, long before the invasion. They'd been looking forward to it for a long time; they had no wish whatever to forego one of their few diversions.

'Didn't I tell you to stop that noise?' Abu-Ali ran out of breath, mopped his forehead.

'He's been like this ever since the invasion,' the schoolteacher whispered to me, 'taken it personally.'

In fact Abu-Ali had been lucky. His three sons, who'd all spent long periods of time in Iraq, were back in Egypt now. The youngest had come back just a month before the invasion. 'People say that God was watching over him,' his mother had said to me when I went into the house to see her. 'They say "you should praise God for bringing him back in time"—as though I didn't know it.'

Abu-Ali had bought a Datsun pick-up truck with his sons' earnings. It was making good money now, ferrying goods between the nearby towns and villages. He had also built apartments for his sons, all of them expensively furnished with the heavy, gilded furniture that was favoured in rural Egypt. Still, there was one more thing he wanted. A car. He had been just about ready to send two of his sons back to Iraq when the war broke out. He'd even bought the tickets.

'That Saddam Hussein,' he said, 'how could anyone know he'd do this?'

I could have told him of a conversation I'd recorded in my diary on 30 September 1980, when I was living down the road in Nashawy. It was a conversation with one of Nabeel's cousins, a bright young medical student, about the Iran–Iraq war:

I asked him whether he thought that after the war Saddam Hussein was going to emerge as the strong man of the Middle East. He said no, he never would, because Egypt's army was the strongest in the Middle East, and perhaps in the world; because Egypt's soldiers were the best in the world!

I could still remember thinking about that exclamation mark.

'That Saddam Hussein,' snarled Abu-Ali. 'I want to kill him.'

His youngest son came into the room and was amazed to see me. After the greetings were over he said: 'Do you know, I used to work for Indians in Iraq? But they were a different kind of Indian—Shia Muslims, Bohras. I used to work in a hotel they ran in Kerbala. It's a great pilgrimage centre you know.'

I was startled: I had only very recently met a group of Bohra Muslims. On my way to Cairo, from Calcutta, I'd had to stop at Amman airport, to catch a connecting flight. I'd met them at the airport. They'd been stranded in Kerbala for several days after the invasion. They'd been very worried, because some members of their party had American and British passports. But when they got to the border it had been all right, the guards had let them through without a word. 'We're Muslims,' they said, 'so it didn't matter.' In Kerbala they'd stayed in a Bohra hotel they'd said— very well run, clean, comfortable. It was an odd coincidence.

'Why did you come through Jordan at a time like this?' he asked. I explained that the trip had been arranged a long time back.

'I travelled through Jordan too once,' he said. 'It was a nice place then. But look at it now. Have you seen the pictures on the TV news? They're frightening. That man. . .'

'I want to kill that Saddam Hussein,' bellowed his father. 'He's spoilt everything.' The thought of that lost car was sawing into his flesh.

'This war's going to be a disaster,' said his son, shaking his head. But he had a look of relief on his face: at least his father wouldn't be able to send him back there now.

'Did you ever come across Nabeel in Iraq?' I asked.

'Nabeel?' he repeated after me. 'Nabeel who?'

'Nabeel Idris Mustafa Badawy,' I said. 'From Nashawy.'

He thought for a moment and shook his head: 'No, I didn't even know he was there. It's a big country and there are so many Egyptians there . . .'

A pick-up truck drew up outside in a flurry of horns. The wash-basins began to crash together, the women began to ululate. The groom had arrived. Abu-Ali paid no notice. He was shouting: '. . . he doesn't know how much harm he's doing to his country. . .'

Many of the men in the room went rushing out to receive the groom. I slipped out with them, unnoticed. Abu-Ali was still shouting: '. . . he has to be killed, as soon as possible.'

Everywhere in Egypt people seemed to be talking of killing. In the taxi out from Cairo, the six passengers had all agreed that Saddam had to be killed. But then somebody had added: 'And what about the Man here? Hasn't he got to go first?' This met with a chorus of approval: 'He's going to die, the Man'; '. . . and if someone wants to kill him, he can count on me for help.'

Never before in Egypt, had I heard ordinary people so much as criticize their President in public, amongst strangers, far less talk of killing him, even if only metaphorically. I looked out of the window, half-expecting the driver to stop the taxi. But soon enough he too was talking of killing—the Iraqis, the Americans, Palestinians, Israelis, Saudis . . .

It was as though the whole country had been startled suddenly out of sleep and fallen out of bed, fists clenched, swinging wildly at everything in sight.

The fact is that it has been a long sleep and on the whole the dreams have been good. So good, that in the dreamtime Egypt has floated away from earth into the upper atmosphere.

For the last few years the principal sources of Egypt's national income have been these: the repatriated earnings of its workers abroad, Western aid and tourism. Oil and fees from the Suez Canal follow, but not close behind. Life above ground—where most countries have their economies—has contributed increasingly little. A few decades ago Egypt used to grow enough food to feed itself and export some too. Since then, in exactly the period in which India and China have gone from dependency to self-sufficiency in food, Egypt has reached a point where it has to import as much as seventy per cent of its grain. To pay for its food it needs foreign exchange. And so tourism has become a desperately serious business, a matter of economic survival.

Minds are hard at work thinking of ways to make Egypt ever more attractive to tourists, ever more fantastic. A year or so ago they hit upon the idea of turning a town into an opera set. Luxor, they decided—the ancient Thebes—would be just the right setting for Verdi's *Aïda*. It needed a fair bit of work to turn a real town and some real ancient Egyptian ruins into an Italian's fantasy of ancient Egypt, but they did a thorough job. Luxor got new roads, new hotels, and miles of brand new wharves along the east bank of the Nile. The wharves are now lined with steamers, often two or three deep: great, floating hotels, several storeys high with many decks of cabins, as well as restaurants, bars, saunas, gyms, swimming-pools. They bring ever-increasing numbers of tourists to Luxor. Last year Egypt had about two million tourists. Almost every single one of them passed through Luxor.

A very large proportion of the tourists come in the steamers. They are taken to the ruins and back again in air-conditioned coaches. The adventurous few take horse-drawn carriages. All the petty difficulties and irritations of travelling in Egypt have been done away with; the only Egyptians the tourists ever encounter are tour guides and waiters (the number is not negligible).

Outside the temple in Karnak is a large notice, prominently displayed. It catches the eye because it is entirely in Arabic. The notices at the monuments are usually in several languages—Arabic, English, French and sometimes even German. But in more ways than one, this notice is not like the others. It contains a list of dos and don'ts for Egyptian visitors—don't make a noise, don't climb the monuments. It ends by exhorting them to behave in a manner 'appropriate to Egyptian culture'. I read it carefully. It makes me think of my aunt in Calcutta, who wanted her money back after visiting the lion sanctuary at the Gir forest in Gujarat. 'Why,' she yelled at the travel agent, 'they were just sleeping, lying in the dust like lizards. Shouldn't someone tell them that they've got to behave like lions?'

I think of stealing the notice, but the tourist police are watching. It seems to me like an icon of the contemporary Middle East: something inestimably precious is found under the earth, and immediately everybody on top is expected to adjust their behaviour accordingly. In this case the pipeline doesn't take anything away; it brings people in, and whisks them through, hermetically sealed.

In the evenings, when a cool breeze blows in from the Nile, the people of Luxor gather on the promenade along the river front. The steamers are brilliantly lit. They are a bit like glass cases at an aquarium: they seem to display entire cross-sections of an ecological niche. The strollers lean over the railings and watch: there's a honeymooning couple, peering nervously from behind the curtains of their cabin, people sitting at the bar, a trim old lady pumping away at a cycling machine, the waiters, watching television. The best time to watch the steamers is dinner time. The tourists file up the stairs, out of the bars and into the dining-room. They sit at their tables, and then the lights are dimmed. Suddenly 'folkloristic troupes' appear, dressed in embroidered fustans, and break into dance. The tourists put down their cutlery and watch the dancers. The strollers lean forward and watch the tourists. Egyptians watching foreigners watching Egyptians dance.

What if the strollers burst into dance, I ask myself. What then?

In the meanwhile the steamers help to keep Egypt's economy afloat. But it would take only one well-aimed blow to push it under—something that would at one stroke send large numbers of Egyptian workers back from the Gulf, put a stop to tourism, and halt the flow of ships through the Suez Canal: something just like the invasion of Kuwait, for example.

On the other hand there would be an increase in Western aid. The seven billion dollar debt for armaments might be cancelled (as it has been). There would be no need for an economy any more. The fantasies of military strength would become real. The whole country would be a weapon, supported by the world outside. Just like Iraq was, for so many years.

3

Fawzia was standing at the door of the new house; she saw me as I turned the corner. 'Nabeel's not back yet, *ya* Amitab,' she said the moment she saw me. 'He's still over there, in Iraq, and here we are sitting here and waiting.'

'Have you had any news from him? A letter?'

'No, nothing,' she said, leading me into their house. 'Nothing at all. The last time we had news of him was when Ismail came back two months ago.'

'Ismail's back?'

'Praise be to God,' she smiled. 'He's back in good health and everything.'

'Where is he?' I said, looking around. 'Can you send for him?'

'Of course,' she said. 'He's just around the corner, sitting at home. He hasn't found a job yet—does odd jobs here and there, but most of the time he has nothing to do. I'll send for him right now.'

I looked around while I waited. Something seemed to have interrupted the work on their house. When I'd last seen it I had had the impression that it would be completed in a matter of months. But now, a year and half later, the floor was still just a platform of packed earth and gravel. The tiles had not been laid yet, and nor had the walls been plastered or painted.

'*Hamdulillah al-salama*,' Ismail was at the door, laughing, his hand extended.

'Why didn't you come?' he said, as soon as the greetings were over. 'You remember that day you telephoned from America? Nabeel telephoned me soon after he'd spoken to you. He just picked up the phone and called me where I was working. He told me that you'd said that you were going to visit us. We expected you, for a long time. We made space in our room, and thought of all the places we'd show you. But you know, Nabeel's boss, the shop-owner? He got really upset—he didn't like it a bit that Nabeel had got a long distance call from America.'

'Why didn't Nabeel come back with you? What news of him?'

'He wanted to come back. In fact he had thought that he would. But then he decided to stay for a few more months, make a little more money, so that they could finish building this house. You see how it's still half-finished—all the money was used up. Prices have gone up this last year, everything costs more.'

'And besides,' said Fawzia, 'what would Nabeel do back here? Look at Ismail—just sitting at home, no job, nothing to do . . .'

Ismail shrugged. 'But still, he wanted to come back. He's been there three years. It's more than most, and it's aged him. You'd see what I mean if you saw him. He looks much older. Life's not easy out there.'

'What do you mean?'

'The Iraqis, you know,' he pulled a face. 'They're wild; all those years of war have made them a little like animals. They come back from the army for a few days at a time, and they go wild, fighting on the streets, drinking. Egyptians never go out on the streets there at night: if some drunken Iraqis came across you they would kill you, just like that, and nobody would even know, for they'd throw away your papers. It's happened, happens all the time. They blame us you see, they say: "You've taken our jobs and our money and grown rich while we're fighting and dying." '

'What about Saddam Hussein?'

'Saddam Hussein!' he rolled his eyes. 'You have to be careful when you breathe that name out there—there are spies everywhere, at every corner, listening. One word about Saddam and you're gone, dead. In those ways it's terrible out there though of course there's the money. But still, you can't live long out there, it's impossible. Did you hear what happened during the World Cup?'

Earlier in the year Egypt had played a football match with Algeria, to decide which team would play in the World Cup. Egypt had won and Egyptians everywhere had gone wild with joy. In Iraq the hundreds of thousands of Egyptians who lived packed together, all of them young, all of them male, with no families, children, wives, nothing to do but stare at their newly bought television sets—they had exploded out of their rooms and into the streets in a delirium of joy. Their football team had restored to them that self-respect that their cassette recorders and television sets had somehow failed to bring. To the Iraqis, who have never had anything like a normal political life, probably never seen crowds except at pilgrimages, the massed ranks of Egyptians must have seemed like the coming of Armageddon. They responded by attacking them on the streets, often with firearms—well-trained in war, they fell upon the jubilant, unarmed crowds of Egyptian workers.

'You can't imagine what it was like,' said Ismail. He had tears in his eyes. 'It was then that I decided to leave. Nabeel decided to leave as well, but of course he always needed to think a long time about everything. At the last minute he thought he'd stay just a little bit longer . . .'

A little later we went to his house to watch the news on the colour television he had brought back with him. It sat perched on its packing case, in the centre of the room, gleaming new, with chickens roosting on a nest of straw beside it. Soon the news started and we saw footage from Jordan: thousands and thousands of men, some in trousers, some in *gallabeyyas*, some carrying their television sets on their backs, some crying out for a drink of water, stretching all the way from the horizon to the Red Sea, standing on the beach as though waiting for the water to part.

There were more than a dozen of us in the room now. We were crowded around the television set, watching carefully, minutely, looking at every face we could see. But there was nothing to be seen except crowds: Nabeel had vanished into the pages of the epic exodus.

FOUAD ELKOURY

THE SUBURBS OF CAIRO

SERPENTINE GALLERY

15 September - 28 October

Edward Ruscha

Kensington Gardens
London, W2 3XA

Recorded information
071 723 9072

9 November 1990 - 6 January 1991

Possible Worlds

SCULPTURE FROM EUROPE

exhibition organised in collaboration with ICA

DON DELILLO
AT YANKEE STADIUM

Here they come, marching into American sunlight. They are grouped in twos, eternal boy-girl, stepping out of the runway beyond the fence in left-center field. The music draws them across the grass, dozens, hundreds, already too many to count. They assemble themselves so tightly, crossing the vast arc of the outfield, that the effect is one of transformation. From a series of linked couples they become one continuous wave, larger all the time, covering the open spaces in navy and white.

Karen's daddy, watching from the grandstand, can't help thinking this is the point. They're one body now, an undifferentiated mass, and this makes him uneasy. He focuses his binoculars on a young woman, another, still another. So many columns set ·so closely. He has never seen anything like this or ever imagined it could happen. He hasn't come here for the spectacle but it is starting to astonish him. They're in the thousands now, approaching division strength, and the old seemly tear-jerk music begins to sound sardonic. Wife Maureen is sitting next to him. She is bold and bright today, wearing candy colours to offset the damp she feels in her heart. Rodge understands completely. They had almost no warning. Grabbed a flight, got a hotel, took the subway, passed through the metal-detector and here they are, trying to comprehend. Rodge is not unequipped for the rude turns of normal fraught experience. He's got a degree and a business and a tax attorney and a cardiologist and a mutual fund and whole life and major medical. But do the assurances always apply? There is a strangeness down there that he never thought he'd see in a ballpark. They take a time-honoured event and repeat it, repeat it, repeat it until something new enters the world.

Look at the girl in the front row, about twenty couples in from the left. He adjusts the eyepiece lever and zooms to max power, hoping to see her features through the bridal veil.

There are still more couples coming out of the runway and folding into the crowd, although crowd is not the right word. He doesn't know what to call them. He imagines they are uniformly smiling, showing the face they squeeze out with the toothpaste every morning. The bridegrooms in identical blue suits, the brides in lace and satin gowns. Maureen looks around at the people in the stands. Parents are easy enough to spot and there are curiosity seekers scattered about, ordinary slouchers and loiterers, others deeper in the mystery, dark-eyed and separate, secretly alert, people who seem to be wearing everything they own, layered and mounded in garments with missing parts, city nomads more strange to her than herdsmen in the Sahel, who at least turn up on the documentary channel. There is no admission fee and gangs of boys roam the far reaches, setting off firecrackers that carry a robust acoustical wallop, barrel bombs and ash cans booming along the concrete ramps and sending people into self-protective spasms. Maureen concentrates on the parents and other relatives, some of the women done up touchingly in best dress and white corsage, staring dead-eyed out of tinted faces. She reports to Rodge that there's a lot of looking back and forth. Nobody knows how to feel and they're checking around for hints. Rodge stays fixed to his binoculars. Six thousand five hundred couples and their daughter is down there somewhere about to marry a man she met two days ago. He's either Japanese or Korean. Rodge didn't get it straight. And he knows about eight words of English. He and Karen spoke through an interpreter, who taught them how to say Hello, it is Tuesday, here is my passport. Fifteen minutes in a bare room and they're chain-linked for life.

He works his glasses across the mass, the crowd, the movement, the membership, the flock, the following. It would make him feel a little better if he could find her.

'You know what it's as though?' Maureen says.

'Let me concentrate.'

'It's as though they designed this to the maximum degree of let the relatives squirm.'

'We can do our moaning at the hotel.'

'I'm simply stating.'

'I did suggest, did I not, that you stay at home.'

'How could I not come? What's my excuse?'

'I see a lot of faces that don't look American. They send them out in missionary teams. Maybe they think we've sunk to the status of less developed country. They're here to show us the way and the light.'

'And make sharp investments. After, can we take in a play?'

'Let me look, OK. I want to find her.'

'We're here. We may as well avail ourselves.'

'It's hard for the mind to conceive. Thirteen thousand people.'

'What are you going to do when you find her?'

'Who the hell thought it up? What does it mean?'

'What are you going to do when you find her? Wave goodbye?'

'I just need to know she's here,' Rodge says. 'I want to document it, OK.'

'Because that's what it is. If it hasn't been goodbye up to this point, it certainly is now.'

'Hey, Maureen? Shut up.'

From the bandstand at home plate the Mendelssohn march carries a stadium echo, with lost notes drifting back from the recesses between tiers. Flags and bunting everywhere. The blessed couples face the infield, where their true father, Master Moon, stands in three dimensions. He looks down at them from a railed pulpit that rides above a platform of silver and crimson. He wears a white silk robe and a high crown figured with stylized irises. They know him at molecular level. He lives in them like chains of matter that determine who they are. This is a man of chunky build who saw Jesus on a mountainside. He spent nine years praying and wept so long and hard his tears formed puddles and soaked through the floor and dripped into the room below and filtered through the foundation of the house into the earth. The couples know there are things he must leave unsaid, words whose planetary impact no one could bear. He is the messianic secret, ordinary-looking, his skin a weathered bronze. When the communists sent him to a labour camp the other inmates knew who he was because they'd dreamed about him before he got there. He gave away half his food but never grew weak. He worked seventeen hours a day in the mines but always found time to pray, to keep his body clean and tuck in his shirt. The blessed couples eat kiddie food and use baby names because they feel so small in his presence. This is a man who lived in a hut made of US Army ration tins and now he is here, in American light, come to lead them to the end of human history.

The brides and grooms exchange rings and vows and many people in the grandstand are taking pictures, standing in the aisles and crowding the rails, whole families snapping anxiously, trying to shape a response or organize a memory, trying to neutralize the event, drain it of eeriness and power. Master chants the ritual in Korean. The couples file past the platform and he sprinkles water on their heads. Rodge sees the brides lift their veils and he zooms in urgently, feeling at the same moment a growing distance from events, a sorriness of spirit. But he watches and muses. When the Old God leaves the world, what happens to all the unexpended faith? He looks at each sweet face, round face, long, wrong, darkish, plain. They are a nation, he supposes, founded on the principle of easy belief. A unit fuelled by credulousness. They speak a half language, a set of ready-made terms and empty repetitions. All things, the sum of the knowable, everything true, it all comes down to a few simple formulas copied and memorized and passed on. And here is the drama of mechanical routine played out with living figures. It knocks him back in awe, the loss of scale and intimacy, the way love and sex are multiplied out, the numbers and shaped crowd. This really scares him, a mass of people turned into a sculptured object. It is like a toy with 13,000 parts, just tootling along, an innocent and menacing thing. He keeps the glasses trained, feeling a slight desperation now, a need to find her and remind himself who she is. Healthy, intelligent, twenty-one, serious-sided, possessed of a selfness, a teeming soul, nuance and shadow, grids of pinpoint singularities they will never drill out of her. Or so he hopes and prays, wondering about the power of their own massed prayer. When the Old God goes, they pray to flies and bottletops. The terrible thing is they follow the man because he gives them what they need. He answers their yearning, unburdens them of free will and independent thought. See how happy they look.

Around the great stadium the tenement barrens stretch, miles of delirium, men sitting in tipped-back chairs against the walls of hollow buildings, sofas burning in the lots, and there is a sense these chanting thousands have, wincing in the sun, that the future is pressing in, collapsing toward them, that they are everywhere surrounded by signs of the fated landscape and human struggle of the Last Days, and here in the middle of their columned body, lank-haired and up-close, stands Karen Janney, holding a cluster of starry jasmine and thinking of the bloodstorm to come. She is waiting to file past Master and sees him with the single floating eye of the crowd, inseparable from her own apparatus of vision but sharper-sighted, able to perceive more deeply. She feels intact, rayed with well-being. They all feel the same, young people from fifty countries, immunized against the language of self. They're forgetting who they are under their clothes, leaving behind all the small banes and body woes, the day-long list of sore gums and sweaty nape and need to pee, ancient rumbles in the gut, momentary chills and tics, the fungoid dampness between the toes, the deep spasm near the shoulder blade that's charged with mortal reckoning. All gone now. They stand and chant, fortified by the blood of numbers.

Karen glances over at Kim Jo Pak, soft-eyed and plump in his nice new suit and boxy shoes, husband-for-eternity.

She knows her flesh parents are in the stands somewhere. Knows what they're saying, sees the gestures and expressions. Dad trying to use old college logic to make sense of it all. Mom wearing the haunted stare that means she was put on earth strictly to suffer. They're all around us, parents in the thousands, afraid of our intensity. This is what frightens them. We really believe. They bring us up to believe but when we show them true belief they call out psychiatrists and police. We know who God is. This makes us crazy in the world.

Karen's mindstream sometimes slows down, veering into sets of whole words. They take a funnny snub-nosed form, the rudimentary English spoken by some of the Master's chief assistants.

They have God once-week. Do not understand. Must sacrifice together. Build with hands God's home on earth.

Karen says to Kim, 'This is where the Yankees play.'

He nods and smiles, blankly. Nothing about him strikes her so forcefully as his hair, which is shiny and fine and ink-black, with a Sunday comics look. It is the thing that makes him real to her.

'Baseball,' she says, using the word to sum up a hundred happy abstractions, themes that flare to life in the crowd shout and diamond symmetry, in the details of a dusty slide. The word has resonance if you're American, a sense of shared heart and untranslatable lore. But she only means to suggest the democratic clamour, a history of sweat and play on sun-dazed afternoons, an openness of form that makes the game a kind of welcome-to-my-country.

The other word is cult. How they love to use it against us. Gives them the false term they need to define us as eerie-eyed children. And how they hate our willingness to work and struggle. They want to snatch us back to the land of lawns. That we are willing to live on the road, sleep on the floor, crowd into vans and drive all night, fund-raising, serving Master. That our true father is a foreigner and nonwhite. How they silently despise. They keep our rooms ready. They have our names on their lips. But we're a lifetime away, weeping through hours of fist-pounding prayer.

World in pieces. It is shock of shocks. But there is plan. Pali-pali. Bring hurry-up time to all man.

She does not dream any more except about Master. They all dream about him. They see him in visions. He stands in the room with them when his three-dimensional body is thousands of miles away. They talk about him and weep. The tears roll down their faces and form puddles on the floor and drip into the room below. He is part of the structure of their protein. He lifts them out of ordinary strips of space and time and then shows them the blessedness of lives devoted to the ordinary, to work, prayer and obedience.

Rodge offers the binoculars to Maureen. She shakes her head firmly. It is like looking for the body of a loved one after a typhoon.

Balloons in clusters rise by the thousands, sailing past the rim of the upper deck. Karen lifts her veil and passes below the pulpit, which is rimmed on three sides by bullet-proof panels. She feels the blast of Master's being, the solar force of a charismatic soul. Never so close before. He sprinkles mist from a holy bottle in her face. She sees Kim move his lips, following Master's chant word for word. She's close enough to the grandstand to see people crowding the rails, standing everywhere to take pictures. Did she ever think she'd find herself in a stadium in New York, photographed by thousands of people? There may be as many people taking pictures as there are brides and grooms. One of them for every one of us. Clickety-click. The thought makes the couples a little giddy. They feel that space is contagious. They're here but also there, already in the albums and slide projectors, filling picture frames with their microcosmic bodies, the minikin selves they are trying to become.

They veer back to the outfield grass to resume formation. There are folk troupes near both dug-outs dancing to gongs and drums. Karen fades into the thousands, the columned mass. She feels the metre of their breathing. They're a world family now, each marriage a channel to salvation. Master chooses every mate, seeing in a vision how backgrounds and characters match. It is a mandate from heaven, pre-ordained, each person put here to meet the perfect other. Forty days of separation before they're alone in a room, allowed to touch and love. Or longer. Or years if Master sees the need. Take cold showers. It is this rigour that draws the strong. Their self-control cuts deep against the age, against the private ciphers, the systems of isolated craving. Husband and wife agree to live in different countries, doing missionary work, extending the breadth of the body common. Satan hates cold showers.

The crowd-eye hangs brightly above them like the triangle eye on a dollar bill.

A firecracker goes off, another M-80 banging out of an exit ramp with a hard flat impact that drives people's heads into their torsos. Maureen looks battle-stunned. There are lines of boys wending through empty rows high in the upper deck, some of them only ten or twelve years old, moving with the princely swagger of famous street felons. She decides she doesn't see them.

'I'll tell you this,' Rodge says. 'I fully intend to examine this organization. Hit the libraries, get on the phone, contact parents, truly delve. You hear about support groups that people call for all kinds of things.'

'We need support. I grant you that. But you're light years too late.'

'I think we ought to change our flight as soon as we get back to the hotel and then check out and get going.'

'They'll charge us for the room for tonight anyway. We may as well get tickets to something.'

'The sooner we get started on this.'

'Raring to go. Oh boy. What fun.'

'I want to read everything I can get my hands on. Only did some skimming but that's because I didn't know she was involved in something so grandiose. We ought to get some hotline numbers and see who's out there that we can talk to.'

'You sound like one of those people, you know, when they get struck down by some rare disease they learn every inch of material they can find in the medical books and phone up doctors on three continents and hunt day and night for people with the same awful thing.'

'Makes good sense, Maureen.'

'They fly to Houston to see the top man. The top man is always in Houston.'

'What's wrong with learning everything you can?'

'You don't have to *enjoy* it.'

'It's not a question of enjoy it. It's our responsibility to Karen.'

'Where is she by the way?'

'I fully intend.'

'You were scanning so duteously. What, bored already?'

A wind springs up, causing veils to rustle and lift. Couples cry out, surprised, caught in a sudden lightsome glide, a buoyancy. They remember they are kids, mostly, and not altogether done with infections of glee. They have a shared past after all. Karen thinks of all those nights she slept in a van or crowded room, rising at five for prayer condition, then into the streets with her flower team. There was a girl named June who felt she was shrinking, falling back to child size. They called her Junette. Her hands could not grip the midget bars of soap in the motel toilets of America. This did not seem unreasonable to the rest of the team. She was only seeing what was really there, the slinking shape of eternity beneath the paint layers and glutamates of physical earth.

All those lost landscapes. Nights downtown, live nude shows in cinderblock bunkers, slums with their dumpster garbage. All those depopulated streets in subdivisions at the edge of Metroplex, waist-high trees and fresh tar smoking in the driveways and nice-size rattlers that cozy out of the rocks behind the last split-level. Karen worked to make the 400 dollar a day standard, peddling mainly bud roses and sweet williams. Just dream-walking into places and dashing out. Rows of neat homes in crashing rain. People drooped over tables at five a.m. at casinos in the desert. Progressive Slot Jackpots. Welcome Teamsters. She fasted on liquids for a week, then fell upon a stack of Big Macs. Through revolving doors into hotel lobbies and department stores until security came scurrying with their walkie-talkies and beepers and combat magnums.

They prayed kneeling with hands crossed at forehead, bowed deep, folded like unborn young.

In the van everything mattered, every word counted, sometimes fifteen, sixteen sisters packed in tight, singing you are my sunshine, row row row, chanting their monetary goal. Satan owns the fallen world.

She stacked bundles of baby yellows in groups of seven, the number-symbol of perfection. There were times when she not only thought in broken English but spoke aloud in the voices of the workshops and training sessions, lecturing the sisters in the van, pressing them to sell, make the goal, grab the cash, and they didn't know whether to be inspired by the uncanny mimicry or report her for disrespect.

Junette was a whirlwind of awe. Everything was too much for her, too large and living. The sisters prayed with her and wept. Water rocked in the flower buckets. They had twenty-one-day selling contests, three hours' sleep. When a sister ran off, they holy-salted the clothes she'd left behind. They chanted, We're the greatest, there's no doubt; heavenly father, we'll sell out.

After midnight in some bar in that winter stillness called the inner city. God's own lonely call. Buy a carnation, sir. Karen welcomed the chance to walk among the lower-downs, the sort of legions of the night. She slipped into semi-trance, detached and martyrish, passing through those bare-looking storefronts, the air jangly with other-mindedness. A number of dug-in drinkers bought a flower or two, men with long flat fingers and pearly nails, awake to the novelty, or hat-wearing men with looks of high scruple, staring hard at the rain-slickered girl. What new harassment they pushing in off the street? An old hoocher told her funny things, a line of sweat sitting on his upper lip. She got the bum's rush fairly often. Don't be so subjective, sir. Then scanned the street for another weary saloon.

Team leader said, Gotta get goin', kids. Pali-pali.

In the van every truth was magnified, everything they said and did separated them from the misery jig going on out there. They looked through the windows and saw the faces of fallen-world people. It totalized their attachment to true father. Pray all night at times, all of them, chanting, shouting out, leaping up from prayer stance, lovely moaning prayers to Master, oh *please*, oh *yes*, huddled in motel room in nowhere part of Denver.

Karen said to them, 'Which you like to sleep, five hour or four?'

FOUR.

She said, 'Which you like to sleep, four hour or three?'

THREE.

She said, 'Which you like to sleep, three hour or none?'

NONE.

In the van every rule counted double, every sister was subject to routine scrutiny in the way she dressed, prayed, brushed her hair, brushed her teeth. They knew there was only one way to leave the van without risking the horror of lifetime drift and guilt. Follow the wrist-slashing fad. Or walk out a high-rise window. It's better to enter grey space than disappoint Master.

Team leader said, Prethink your total day. Then jump it,

jump it, jump it.

Oatmeal and water. Bread and jelly. Row row row your boat. Karen said to them, Lose sleep, it is for sins. Lose weight, it is for sins. Lose hair, lose nail off finger, lose whole hand, whole arm, it go on scale to stand against sins.

The man in Indiana who ate the rose she sold him.

Racing through malls at sundown to reach the daily goal. Blitzing the coin laundries and bus terminals. Door to door in police dog projects, saying the money's for drug centres ma'am. Junette kidnapped by her parents in Skokie, Illinois. Scotch-taping limp flowers to make them half-way saleable. Crazy weather on the plains. Falling asleep at meals, heavy-eyed, dozing on the toilet, sneaking some Z's, catching forty winks, nodding off, hitting the hay, crashing where you can, flaked-out, dead to the world, sleep like a top, like a log, desperate for some shut-eye, some sack time, anything for beddy-bye, a cat nap, a snooze, a minute with the sandman. Prayer condition helped them jump it to the limit, got the sorry blood pounding. Aware of all the nego media, which multiplied a ton of doubt for less committed sisters. Doing the hokey-pokey. Coldest winter in these parts since they started keeping records. Chanting the monetary goal.

Team leader said, Gotta hurry hurry hurry. Pali-pali, kids.

Rodge sits there in his rumpled sport coat, pockets crammed with travellers cheques, credit cards and subway maps, and he looks through the precision glasses, and looks and looks, and all he sees is repetition and despair. They are chanting again, one word this time, over and over, and he can't tell if it is English or some other known language or some football holler from heaven. No sign of Karen. He puts down the binoculars. People are still taking pictures. He half expects the chanting mass of bodies to rise in the air, all 13,000 ascending slowly to the height of the stadium roof, lifted by the picture-taking, the forming of aura, radiant brides clutching their bouquets, grooms showing sunny teeth. A smoke bomb sails out of the bleachers, releasing a trail of Day-Glo fog.

Master leads the chant, *Mansei*, ten thousand years of victory. The blessed couples move their lips in unison, matching

223

the echo of his amplified voice. There is stark awareness in their faces, a near pain of rapt adoration. He is Lord of the Second Advent, the unriddling of many ills. His voice leads them out past love and joy, past the beauty of their mission, out past miracles and surrendered self. There is something in the chant, the fact of chanting, the being-one, that transports them with its power. Their voices grow in intensity. They are carried on the sound, the soar and fall. The chant becomes the boundaries of the world. They see their Master frozen in his whiteness against the patches and shadows, the towering sweep of the stadium. He raises his arms and the chant grows louder and the young arms rise. He leads them out past religion and history, thousands weeping now, all arms high. They are gripped by the force of a longing. They know at once, they feel it, all of them together, a longing deep in time, running in the earthly blood. This is what people have wanted since consciousness became corrupt. The chant brings the End Time closer. The chant is the End Time. They feel the power of the human voice, the power of a single word repeated as it moves them deeper into oneness. They chant for world-shattering rapture, for the truth of prophecies and astonishments. They chant for new life, peace eternal, the end of soul-lonely pain. Someone on the bandstand beats a massive drum. They chant for one language, one word, for the time when names are lost.

Karen, strangely, is daydreaming. It will take some getting used to, a husband named Kim. She has known girls named Kim since she was a squirt in a sunsuit. Quite a few really. Kimberleys and plain Kims. Look at his hair gleaming in the sun. My husband, weird as it sounds. They will pray together, whole-skinned, and memorize every word of Master's teaching.

The thousands stand and chant. Around them in the world, people ride escalators going up and sneak secret glances at the faces coming down. People dangle tea-bags over hot water in white cups. Cars run silently on the autobahns, streaks of painted light. People sit at desks and stare at office walls. They smell their shirts and drop them in the hamper. People bind themselves into numbered seats and fly across time zones and high cirrus and deep night, knowing there is something they've forgotten to do.

The future belongs to crowds.

GRANTA BOOKS

Martha Gellhorn
The View from the Ground

Martha Gellhorn's peacetime dispatches bear witness to six decades of change: America in the Great Depression, the betrayal of Czechoslovakia, Christmas with the unemployed in London, the trial of Adolf Eichmann, Spain in the days after Franco's death, Cuba revisited after forty-one years. Here is history as it looked and felt to the people who lived through it.

'An eloquent, unforgettable history of a chaotic century.'
San Francisco Chronicle

'Martha Gellhorn's writing is spiked with intelligence, individualism and moral indignation.'
New Statesman & Society

'Gellhorn's work is infused by passion as James Cameron said that all great reporting should be.'
Scotsman

'A sharp, eye, a retentive memory and a sparse, powerful prose.'
Sunday Telegraph

'Deep with humanity and beautifully written.'
Guardian

Hardback, 480 pages £14.95 ISBN 0140-14200-2
October paperback publication

MARTIN AMIS
TIME'S ARROW

W here do they go, these little ones who disappear—the uncreated? Safely curled inside their mothers, for a while; but then what? I have an intractable presentiment (maybe a hope, maybe a fear) that one night I will glimpse them, in Tod's dream . . . Some mornings, as we prepare to turn in, and go through the heavy routines, of mussing, of miring, we can feel the dream just waiting to happen, gathering its energies from somewhere on the other side. We're fatalistic. We make no attempt to go to sleep. We lie there, with the lamp burning, while dawn fades. In quickening series, tepid sweats slowly form, and briefly shine, and instantly evaporate. Later, Tod's heart rate begins to steepen: even his ears thump with the new blood. There follows a timeless and pitiable period of steadily worsening confusion. By now the bed reeks of fear. I have to be ready for when Tod makes his lurch for the light-switch. And then, in darkness, with a hot shout which gives a savage twist to his jaw—we're in it. The dream. We're in it right up to our neck. The enormous figure in the white coat, his black boots straddling many acres. Somewhere down there, between his legs, the queues of souls. I wish I had power, just power enough to avert my eyes. Please, don't show me the babies! . . . Where does the dream come from? It must come from the future. The dream must be about what Tod will someday do.

It's mildly encouraging, now, in the street, when Tod looks at a woman. For once his eyes point where I want them to point. Our priorities or imperatives are by no means identical, but at least they overlap. We like the same kind of woman—the womanly kind. All ages. Now, Tod looks first at the face; then the breasts; then the lower abdomen. If it's a back view, we go: hair; waist; rump. Neither of us, it would seem, is much of a leg man—though I could do with a bit more than I get. Another thing bothers me: the timespots Tod allows for each section. Tod is done with the face way too soon. A single downward swipe of the eyes. Whereas I'd like to linger. Maybe the etiquette forbids this. Still, I'm mildly encouraged. There's hardly any of the usual vertigo effect, when I'm trying to see things that he's not looking at, when I'm trying to look at things he's not seeing.

Vivified, perhaps, by all this fieldwork we're doing, our

solitary sex sessions have become a lot livelier of late. The missing component, the extra essence is generated, of course, by the toilet, by the trash. You just daub it on. And you're away.

Where would Tod and I be without the toilet? Where would we be without all the trash?

There is a thing out there called *fashion*. The young observe it. In footwear, headwear, eyewear; the experiments in mortification they perform on their own faces—the piercings, the pallor. Are they telling the story of the armoured dinosaurs, in chronological miniature, with horns of hair and collars of hide? Fashion is for youth and all its volatility, but Tod and I occasionally dabble. For instance, we went to the Thrift Store and got given two pairs of flared pants. Naturally I wanted to try them on right away; but for months he let them languish in the closet upstairs, growing the wrinkles and airpockets that would eventually fit his shape, the peculiar wishbone of his shanks. Then, one night, he unceremoniously slipped into them. Later, after work, I got a pretty good look at these new pants of ours, as Tod stood before the full-length mirror, unknotting his tie. Well, they weren't actually outrageous, Tod's flares, nothing like the twin-ballgown effect we would soon start seeing on the street. But I found them thoroughly disgraceful, all the same: aesthetically, they worked on me like violence. This packed, cuboid, still elderly party (always growing, always getting stronger)—and his slobbering calves. Where have his *feet* gone, for Christ's sake? I knew then, I think, that Tod's cruelty, his secret, had to do with a central mistake about people's bodies. Or maybe I just discovered something about the style or the *line* of his cruelty. Tod's cruelty would be trashy, shitty, mistaken, bassackward: flared . . . Still, the pants caught on and now everyone is into them. They move down the street like yachts—the cashiered, the landlocked sailors of the city! Next thing you know, women's hemlines go up by about three feet. The sudden candour and power of female haunch. They're already coming down again, slowly, but Jesus.

A war is coming. Just a little one, for now. I'm intellectually prepared for it, I suppose—I suppose I'm as ready as I'll ever be.

Several times now, in bars, looking up briefly from our Bud or our Molson or our San Mig, we have seen that same shot on the mounted TV: like a eugenic cross between swordfish and stingray, the helicopter twirls upward from the ocean and crouches grimly on the deck of the aircraft carrier, ready to fight. War nears, with all its violence and renewal. To the question of violence (this most difficult question), certain answers will no doubt be offered. The streets churn and wait, but celebrations are so far muted.

On arising to start the day, around midnight, perhaps, when he's still drunk, Tod Friendly will create things. Wildly he will mend and heal. Taking hold of the woodwork and the webbing, with a single blow to the floor, with a single impact, he will create a kitchen chair. With one fierce and skilful kick of his aching foot he will mend a deep concavity in the refrigerator's side. With a butt of his head he will heal the fissured bathroom mirror, heal also the worsening welt in his own forehead, and then stand there staring at himself with his eyes flickering.

A t last. Give thanks. Give thanks. It's started to happen. Oh my God, I think I love her.

Irene didn't catch me completely on the hop—I had fair warning. The arrival of my lovelife was preceded by the arrival of a whole new bunch of loveletters. But these weren't loveletters from Irene. These were loveletters *to* Irene. Written by Tod. In his squat and unvarying hand. They came from the trash, of course, from the innards of a ten-gallon Hefty: we bent over the bag and kind of airlifted them out of there. Then Tod went and sat in the living room with this red-ribboned bundle on his lap. He got his blue tin out too. We sat there for about a half hour. The suspense was killing me. Finally Tod took a letter from the middle of the stack, opened it out and stared at it with an unfocused, an uncommitted eye. I took in what I could. 'My dear Irene, Thank you again for the cushions. I *do* like them. They brighten up the room, as well as making it more "cosy" . . . Give the key to Johnson and if he isn't there never mind until next time . . . You must not get obsessed by this matter of your veins, which are fairly superficial (no pigmentation, no edema). If you are decided then of course I will help but remember I like you just the way you are . . . I look forward with the usual impatience to seeing you on Tuesday though Friday might be better . . .' Blankly Tod removed the letters from his lap and replaced them with that tin of his, in which, after a pause, he began to rootle. The photograph Tod wanted was all creased and bent but he soon healed it with a firm squeeze of his fist. Wow, I thought. So I guess that's the one. No spring chicken. Not by any means. And a really *big* old broad. Smiling, in a tan pants suit. When he left for work that evening Tod left the letters by the front step, encased in a white shoebox on which someone—presumably Irene—had scrawled the words FUCK YOU. It didn't seem like an awfully good sign.

Nine nights later we woke up in the small hours and lay there coldly. 'Shtib,' he grunted. Tod's been doing this quite a bit lately—grunting: Shtib. Shtib. I thought it might be a cough, or a half-suppressed eructation, or just some unalluring new vagary. Then I realized what it was the guy was saying. He climbed out of bed and opened the window: in stages, in subtle gusts, the room began to fill with the warmth and spoor of an alien being. Most noticeably, and surprisingly, cigarette smoke!—which Tod has a big thing about. Also something pastelike and candyish, something sweet and old. These were the smells she was sending across the city. Oh boy: here we go. Come to me baby. Unhurriedly Tod climbed out of his pajamas and donned his fibrous dressing-gown. As he discomposed the bedding I noticed that my feeling tone was markedly at variance with his: his was resigned, unengaged, inconvenienced. Still, at least he prepared her cigarettes for her, filling a saucer with a couple of butts and plenty of ash. We shut the window and went downstairs and waited.

It showed good form—and was, I thought, rather romantic of Tod—to go outside like that and stand in his slippers on the wet sidewalk. Very soon we heard her car, its slithering approach, and saw the twin red lights at the end of the street. She parked, and opened the car door loudly, and jumped out. She walked *forward* across the road, shaking her head in sorrow or denial. A really big old broad. Irene. Yeah.

'Tod?' she said. 'This is it. Happy now?'

Happy or not, Tod preceded her through the front door. She

wrenched off her coat while Tod went on up, and then she
pounded after him. I was discouraged, I have to admit. I guess
I'd been hoping it would all be beautiful—that there would be
sweet words. But no. I have to go and catch her on a really bad
day. Tod and I reclined on the wrung bedding as Irene advanced
into the room, swiping a hand at her streaming eyes and calling
us a piece of shit.

Then she started taking her clothes off. Women!

'Irene,' Tod reasoned.

She undressed quickly; but the speed of her movements had
nothing to do with avidity, with desire. She talked quickly too,
and wept, and shook her head. A big old broad, in big white
sweater, big white pants. Her breasts formed a sharp bluff
beneath her chin, triangular and aerodynamic, kept aloft,
ultimately, by a kind of GI Joe backpack of straps and winches.
Off came the armour, the chainmail of her girdle. Then that big
white tush was ambling toward me. And I thought her *clothes*
were white. What was she saying, Irene, what was she going on
about, in words half heard, half drowned—in gasps and
whispers? In summary, this: that men were either too dumb or
too sharp with nothing in between. Too dumb or too sharp. Too
innocent, too guilty. Tod, at any rate, listened to her in frank
exasperation, his nostrils tensely flared, his upper lip shaped like
a mean little beak.

'Mean?' he began. 'You live in your body. And now the
body is giving out.'

She flung herself down beside me, awkwardly, abundantly.
Tod's words seemed to have a relaxing effect on her. I placed an
arm around the white pulp of her shoulder.

Irene said in a frightened voice, 'What's that supposed to
mean?'

'All night, too.'

'I make allowances,' she said. 'You deal with the sick all
day.'

'That's something you don't ever talk about.'

'Were there kids?'

'That's something you don't ever talk about.'

'Were you this nice to your wife?'

'Well. We wouldn't know about that, would we, Irene.'

'Except to your friends. Your loved ones.'

'You have no obligation to be healthy.'

'Also fatal.'

'Do you really have to do that? It's a disgusting habit.'

Tod started coughing and flapping his thick right hand about. After a while she quenched the cigarette of its fire and restored it to the pack. She turned toward us. There followed about ten minutes of what you'd call foreplay. Snuggling, grunting, sighing—that kind of thing. Then the act happened . . . And I thought: That's it?

Afterward, it was all so very much easier. The atmosphere was first rate as we put our clothes back on and went downstairs to have something to eat. There we sat, side by side at the dinette feature, equably untwirling yard upon yard of the pale pasta. Then—another first—off to the movies! This passed off fine also. I was worried at first, when Irene started crying again before we had even taken our seats and I suppose the film was pretty depressing. All about love. The on-screen couple, quietly glowing with beauty and amusement—they seemed made for each other; but after various misunderstandings and adventures and other nonsense, they ended up going their separate ways. By this time Irene was emitting a faint gurgle of pleasure, when she wasn't laughing her head off. Everyone was laughing. But not Tod. Not Tod. Actually, I didn't think it was funny either. We ended up at a bar. Irene had Old Fashioneds. Tod with his steins. Our parting was marked by its cordiality and affection. I know I'm going to be seeing a lot more of her. We have our problems, clearly, but they're nothing we can't handle. On top of which I came out thirty-three dollars to the good. Make that thirty six with the popcorn.

Success. I loved it. Irene's great. All that day at work I had a mellow feeling about her. In the small hours, there, I experienced some initial alarm, but she looked better and better as the date progressed. Such humanity in her young eyes, peeping out in embarrassment from behind the worn sneaker of her face, so puffed, so pinched, so parched. It seems to me that you need a lot of courage, or a lot of something, to enter into other people.

We all think that everyone else lives in fortresses, in fastnesses: behind moats, behind steep walls studded with spikes and broken glass. But in fact we inhabit much punier structures. You can just stick your head under the flap of the tent and crawl right in. If you get the OK. So perhaps escape is possible: escape from the— from the indecipherable monad. But I still don't know if Tod will ever really come across.

You'd think it might be quite relaxing, having (effectively) no will, and no body anyway through which to express it. Many administrative and executive matters, it's true, are taken right out of your hands. But there is always the countervailing desire to put yourself forward, to make your mark or your stand as the valuable exception. We all yearn to believe in the religion of the will.

I don't want to sound too flame-eyed and martyr-browed about it—and I know I'm a real simp in many other areas—but I reckon I'm way ahead of Tod on this basic question of human *difference*. Tod has a sophisticated sensing mechanism which guides his responses to all recognizable subspecies. His feeling tone jolts into various attitudes and readinesses: a more or less affable condescension towards Hispanics and Latinos, a mild disgust for Asians, a settled neutrality when it comes to Arabs of any kind; the old Red Indian who drains Tod's tank at the gas station inspires a morbid relish. His most emphatic predispositions concern blacks and Jews. Blacks inspire hatred and rigorous contempt; he'll call them special names under his breath—like jig or schwartzer or boogie. Jews, too, affect him violently, though he has no special names for Jews. And of course he has a secondary repertoire of alerted hostility toward pimps, hookers, junkies, the insane, the club-footed, the hare-lipped, the homosexual male, and the very old.

I've had to learn up on all these distinctions. Originally at least, I had no preselected feelings about anybody, one way or the other (except about doctors: now where did *that* come from?). I know this'll sound unbearably cute, but it took me a while to realize that all negroes have black skin; I was more interested in their eyes, their tongues, the way they moved. When I meet people, I look for a pulse from their inner being, which tells me things like—how much fear, how much hate, how much calm, how much forgiveness. I suppose I really am the soulful type. Visualize the body I don't have, and see this: a sentimentalized foetus, with saintly smile. Naturally, women and children draw forth a reliable response from me, something long preprogrammed. Particularly children, with their purged look, with knowledge being slowly wiped from the mind. All that remains is the ecstasy of the body.

Oh yeah. There's this one guy at AMS, who's Japanese, over from Osaka on a six-month exchange. Companionable enough at first, he's getting less and less relaxed. We call him Mikio: funny-looking kid. During his lunchbreak, in the commissary there, Mikio will sit hunched over a book. I've watched him. He reads the way I read—or *would* read, if I ever got the chance. Mikio begins at the beginning and ends at the end. This makes a kind of quirky sense to me—but Mikio and I are definitely in the minority here. How can we two be right? It would make so many others wrong. Water moves upward. It seeks the highest level. What did you expect? Smoke falls. Things are created in the violence of fire. That's all right. Gravity still pins us to the planet. I'm not sure I'd say anything to Mikio anyway, even if I could, even if I had the power. What *is* it with him? His light-holding hair. His coated eyeballs and their meniscus of severe understanding. No—include me out. Go your own way, pal. I don't want to get involved. Not with that little spook.

Many co-workers—Tod included—razz him about it and everything, but Mikio is free to do this, to read in his own way. People are free, then, they are generally free, then, are they? Well they don't *look* free. Tipping, staggering, with croaked or choking voices, blundering backwards along lines seemingly already crossed, already mapped, never looking where they are going, they move through something prearranged, armed with lies. They're always looking forward to going places they've just come back from, or regretting doing things they haven't yet done. All kings of crap and trash. Signs say No Littering—but who to? We wouldn't dream of it. Government does that, at night, with

trucks; or uniformed men come at morning with their trolleys,
dispensing rubbish, and shit for the dogs.

Rather as I feared they would, babies have started showing
up in Tod's dream. They've shown up. Or, at least, one
of them has: one baby. Nothing gruesome happens and I
am dealing with it fine so far.

You naturally associate babies with helplessness, with
fragility, with enervation; but that's not how it is in the dream.
In the dream, this baby wields appalling power. It has the power,
the ultimate power of life and death over its parents, its older
brothers and sisters, its grandparents, and indeed everybody else
who is gathered in the room. There are about thirty of them in
there, although the room, if it is a room, can't be much bigger
than Tod's kitchen. The room is dark. No, more than this: the
room is black. Despite the power it wields, the baby, curiously
enough, is weeping; perhaps the baby weeps precisely because of
this sinister reversal of authority—the new and desperate
responsibilities it brings. In the faintest of whispers the parents
try to give comfort, try to quieten: for a moment it seems that
they might even have to stifle. There is that excruciating
temptation. Because the baby's drastic ascendancy has to do with
its voice: not its fat fists, its useless legs, but its voice, the sounds
it makes, its capacity to weep. As usual, the parents have the
power of life and death over the baby, as all parents do. But
now, in these special circumstances and in this special room, the
baby has the power over them. And over everybody else who is
gathered there. As I said, about thirty souls.

The whole process is a lot tougher on Tod than it is on me. I'm
always awake when the dreams happen. And I am innocent . . . The
sick shine of an impostor reality, the aura of complicated
accusation—I don't get that. I just settle back, admittedly with
some apprehension, and give witness to the late show screened by
Tod's head, by his hidden mind—by his future. When the time
comes to experience the things that Tod's dreams foretell (when
we find out, for instance, how the baby came to have such
power), then maybe I will take it harder than him. Occasionally,

nowadays, Irene is around to gee Tod up before he goes in there.

I have to say that in physical terms Tod and I are now feeling absolutely terrific. Never better. In the morning, before the mirror, as I inspect Tod's humanity—he shows no sign of noticing the improvement. Me, I want to click my heels, I want to clench my fist: '*Yes*.' Why aren't people happier about how comparatively great they're feeling? Why don't we hug each other all the time, saying, 'How *about* this?'

On the rooftop, on the TV, on the ledge, high up, the crying man in the white shirt, holding the baby. Nearby, a policeman, urgently crouched, all cocked and bunched for this urgent encounter or transaction. The cop is saying that he wants to take the baby. In effect, he wants to disarm the crying man. The crying man has no weapon. The baby is the weapon.

That's not how things stand in the black room, with its groping carbon and tracery, its stilled figures. I just know this. In here, the baby is not a weapon. In here, the baby is more like a bomb.

GRANTA

NOTES FROM ABROAD

In Soweto
Jeremy Harding

T he war came to Soweto along the railway line. On a cold winter morning in August a large party of Inkatha fighters massed on Inhlanzane railway station in Soweto and attacked the five-thirty from Naledi as it pulled in, full of hungover commuters on their way to Johannesburg and young ANC militants swaying between the seats on their routine business of consciousness raising. The first reports coming through gave four dead; the next nine, but by then the dead were already lost in the growing figure for the township as a whole. It could have been worse, but no one was sure how many had been injured at the railway station, and injuries in this war of hacking and slicing and setting alight could be as bad as death.

By mid-morning, a few hours after the attack on the train, a large crowd of residents had massed outside the Jabulani single men's hostel and another outside the hostel in Mapetla. Both places were isolated barracks for Zulu migrant workers deep in the enemy territory of Soweto. There were several such hostels; their occupants lived like a slave labour force, exclusively male, more than six hours drive from their kin, surrounded by the most sophisticated, criminal township culture in southern Africa. When Inkatha made trouble elsewhere, these occupants in Soweto were the objects of bad feeling. Today the trouble was right in the township, building up as the thick brown smog from the night fires started to lift.

Photo: Ken Oosterbroek

241

*M*y first stop was at the house of an acquaintance in Orlando East. Judo Mawisa was in the shebeen. A slight man in his forties with a damaged eye, he came padding out and up to the house and then led me across the township to the Jabulani hostel, near the railway station. As we approached, we encountered barricades put up by the township residents. There had been a clash between young residents and Inkatha but no one seemed certain of the outcome. People were preparing for the next round. A woman in her mid-forties launched a barrage of rhetoric against Inkatha for the benefit of a BBC reporter. She was an eloquent figure in a bright dress who evoked the virtues of the old Soweto. A crowd of younger women stood around, cheering her on. 'The hostel system is a creation of apartheid,' she said. 'We must finish with apartheid for good.' This was true; it was also a discreet way of saying that the hostels should be torched, and Inkatha with them. When the reporter had switched off his tape machine, she straightened her dress and the younger women applauded her.

An adolescent in ripped check trousers and a wide-collared shirt said there was trouble at the hostel in Mapetla and ordered me to take him there. Mapetla was a mile and a bit along the railway line from Inhlanzane, at Merafe station. A deep scar ran across the bridge of the boy's nose as far as his left jaw-bone. Was he an ANC militant? Or a thug? Or someone who had spent too long in detention? In Soweto you could be all these things.

The dust patch which separated the area around the hostel from the rest of Mapetla was occupied by security forces. The area was the size of a football ground. A yellow police van was dropping yards of concertina wire across the front of the hostel. The van came to a stop and two policemen got out to look at the wire. Inkatha too, about forty of them, were watching from behind the barrier. Their clothes were ragged and dirty. They wore red headbands and carried home-made weapons: axes, sharpened pipes, swords, knives, *pangas* and spears. One or two had traditional shields made of hide. There was not enough wire to stop a confrontation between Inkatha and the township residents assembled at the opposite side of the dust patch. It was merely a question of who moved first.

After a time Inkatha started to sing dance the coarse martial dances I had seen before outside the Zulu hostels in Johannesburg. A single dancer came forward, leaped, squatted, spun impeccably in his torn T-shirt and flared trousers and fell to the dusty ground. Then he stood up wearing an expression of calm and made way for another dancer. The main body of men was chanting and beating the plastic covers of the makeshift vendors' sheds behind the razor wire. I walked closer to the wire and stood beside two black policemen. At one time or another, most people had watched Zulus dance for recreation, but this was another matter. One of the policemen smiled, folding his arms in a show of indifference. The BBC reporter trudged past us and up to the wire with his microphone held out in front of him, like a divining-rod.

The effect of the dance was to rally all the participants up to the edge of the wire where, they then threatened to spill over on to the dust patch. The police then moved up, preparing to contain them. On the other side, at the far edge of the hostel, a disorderly mass of warriors had emerged and was marching on the residents. There was no razor wire to stop it, and it had already reached the dust patch.

How many Zulus were there? A hundred? Two hundred? You couldn't tell; they were packed together and were led by a single warrior twenty feet ahead of them, moving in a crouched position, knees bent, head and neck thrust forward. He was brandishing a *panga* in his right hand, high over the concave sweep of his back; his left hand trailed in the dust.

Two white policemen in uniform raced across the dust patch, knelt and fired tear-gas charges at the head of the medieval army and dozens of tall silhouettes writhed in the smoke. When they emerged, the Inkatha ranks had broken and retreated to the hostel; now the residents advanced into the thinning tear-gas. About a hundred of them, led by young men armed with knives

An Inkatha war party, Tokoza, August 1990.

Photo: Ken Oosterbroek

and clubs, were striding over the dust patch like angry nineteenth-century workers marching on a mill.

T he idea that the police were as much a part of the problem as they had been in Natal seemed a facile view of the bloodshed. The ANC clung to it with a stubborn loyalty that was an obstacle to peace. Or so I imagined. ANC dignitaries would fire off volleys of blame at the security forces, which smacked of retribution—a good way to ensure that sins went on being committed. In Bochabela Street, however, I began to see that sins were sins and that it scarcely mattered whether they were new or old.

A young ANC member had guided us up from the hostel in Mapetla towards Jabulani. The route was a maze of barricaded streets, full of residents ebbing away from the confrontation of minutes earlier. In the tart, stinging air they pulled up their shirts or pullovers to cover their faces. The police had spent more tear-gas on them than they had on Inkatha, and had given pursuit. Bochabela Street was half a mile across the railway line from the Jabulani hostel. The simple barricade of large rocks at the bottom of the street was opened up for us and closed again by a group of children. The top end of the street was on fire.

A white minibus, full of uniformed police firing tear-gas and rubber bullets, came down the street and broke up the barricade at the bottom. The young residents vanished. After a minute or more, they regrouped and threw some rocks. The minibus hurtled down again, discharging tear-gas. Crouching in the yard of the shebeen, I was suddenly caught in a different war—the old war of grievance between the state and the disenfranchised townships. It was the one which the suspension of the armed struggle had failed to end.

In Bochabela Street, the conflict with Inkatha was forgotten in the intensity of a confrontation with the security forces. Yet for the residents the skirmish had a lassitude about it—this dismal coming and going through the smoke was in strict accordance with established codes: the barricade, the crude projectile, the smouldering fires of vigilance, the cloth over the mouth. The police went through the ritual moves with far more conviction. They had made four or five runs down the street now and it was all but clear. They had only to refrain from another and the battle would be finished. But apparently absolute silence on Bochabela Street was the only acceptable outcome. Just as you thought it was all over, a single young man would cross the road or a child would dart its head out of a yard gate and this would be enough to bring a hail of gas and rubber bullets from the minibus. At length the minibus did its final run. It shot off a single tear-gas cartridge—presumably for luck, because the street was empty. The children were inside with the women, the injured had been hauled over the wall into Limakatso Street and the fire at the top of the road was dying down.

*O*n Friday in Johannesburg, the press were waiting for news of a peace forum mooted by the Soweto police. Local leaders from Inkatha and the ANC would calm their supporters and peace would return. By eleven o'clock the initiative had failed. The war was already out of hand. In less than a week, 150 people had died and 1,000 had been injured. There had been fighting around the hostel in Mapetla during the night. At three in the morning a band of Inkatha had crept from the hostel and hacked a resident to death with *pangas* in her yard. Mrs Lenah Modibedi was seventy-two. Militants from the ANC later caught a Zulu—a plausible Inkatha—whom they stabbed and set alight.

Today's Great Fire had dug a black tunnel into the sky above Jabulani. It was not at the hostel but the quarters of the municipal police. A hole had been smashed in the concrete perimeter and the residents were peering through at a burning dump of waste and rubber. Someone said the police had started the fire to deflect attention from the hostel. Others said it was the work of the young residents who were now on top of the railway

Police water cannon in Soweto.

Photo: Ken Oosterbroek

cutting half a mile away, starting another.

Judo led me into a nearby house to confront a small man standing in silence beside an upright green sofa with a large oval burn on one of its arms. The floor was covered with plastic stuffing, water and glass. The man was looking through the broken window and scarcely noticed our arrival. He was oblivious to the residue of tear-gas in the room. Judo's one good eye began to water. I stumbled out to the back snivelling and spitting. A woman was leaning against the yard wall, surveying a spread of burned, waterlogged cushions.

By late afternoon the death toll in Soweto had climbed. There was a grim stand-off between Zulus and residents in Mapetla; the police had killed two people already: an unidentified petrol bomber and an innocent teenager. The police, it seemed, had also come under fire from residents with live rounds somewhere in the township. The armed struggle was suspended by a fine thread.

An attack in Jabavu, across the railway line from the Jabulani hostel, drew us back there. It was unclear what had happened; the explanations of the residents were confused. One account subsided under the weight of another; two rival versions collapsed into a third; no one could agree on how it went. If the dead man could have risen from the ground to tell his story, someone would have contradicted him. And then he would have been arrested.

A group of Inkatha had left the Jabulani hostel, crossing the railway line some distance from the bridge; crept down through the bushes and came round by a little path to mount an attack. There were several of them, but the witnesses were not sure quite how many. Neither were they sure who had died.

Two residents, yes, that was it.

Had some of the bodies already been taken away?

Yes, residents' bodies, the bodies of our own young men. But wait, some Inkatha were also killed in the confrontation. Inkatha, they said, were armed with AK47s.

Photo: Ken Oosterbroek

That was a bad sign. How had the guns got into the hostels, if not through some channel of the security forces?

Inkatha had its own sources in Natal, they said, but up here a hostel dweller couldn't come by a Kalashnikov without help.

There was a thick crush of residents at the top of the path and the police, dozens of police, were trying not to be drawn into the argument about whether there had been gunfire. There had been none, they said, and that was the end of it.

The residents insisted; someone alleged that the gunfire had come from the bridge, not from the raiding party on the path.

No, said the police, that was impossible.

The residents pressed forward, remonstrating, shouting, holding out their hands in support of arguments that could only lead them further into the exasperation of their own lives.

The police stood back with their weapons at their sides or slung from their shoulders. Some of them looked decent enough, but this war was conspicuously short of goodness or consistency. A policeman could behave like a professional until dusk and then go his own way—with Inkatha, perhaps—after dark. A young resident could speak out to the press about the evils of the necklace and then incinerate a Zulu once the news crews had retired at sunset with a story from the township. A figurehead in Inkatha could condemn the violence with great conviction and, in the next breath, incite it.

*T*he body of Richard Lebona was stretched out in the dusty little track that led around to the railway. It was covered from the shins to the head with a synthetic blanket woven in drab, ersatz tartan. The head was poised on a few pages of bloody newsprint. Richard Lebona had almost certainly been shot but it scarcely mattered now. Under the blanket there might be stab wounds or bullet wounds. Whoever cared to argue the point at length would have to wade across the fact of the death to the cold banks of conjecture—or pull away the blanket.

Two middle-aged women wearing berets sat in silence beside

the body, raising one hand now and again to their faces. The thick, grieving fingers brushed mechanically against each dry cheek. A vehicle arrived and a pair of orderlies removed an aluminium stretcher. The women watched in silence. It was a clumsy operation. The orderlies heaved at Richard Lebona's body; the newspaper stuck to the hair, rose from the ground and fell back once more as the head jerked stiffly away from the blanket. A drop of damp blood, poised above the upper lip, rolled back into the dead man's nostril. When the stretcher was lifted into the van, the women broke their silence, wailing, imploring, rising to their feet and holding out their arms towards the body. The doors closed and the vehicle pulled away. They set off weeping behind it.

I shared a bed that night with Judo in a house in Jabulani, a mile and a half from the place where Richard Lebona was shot, or otherwise despatched, by Inkatha. Dlangamandla Street—the name meant 'Eat with Power'—was a stone's throw from a big cemetery. We had walked past it in the darkness and one of the young men who was with us took me by the elbow, explaining that we were safe on this stretch of road: ordinary thugs, and probably Inkatha too, were afraid to venture here at night because of the dead. 'Only the rats,' he said, 'are moving on this street in darkness. The rats from the cemetery.' Fourteen years ago, at a turning point in the history of apartheid, the school children of Soweto had marched on this vast graveyard. Everything had appeared much simpler then. There were the forces of apartheid and there were those who opposed it. Now, in the first light of the liberation, Soweto was opaque and murderous.

We listened to the radio with a Zulu by the name of Wide World, in a house on the next street. The news put the day's death toll in the township at thirty-five. On 16 June 1976 not even half that number had been killed. People rarely spoke of the Soweto massacre any more. It was as though a shadow had fallen between them and their past. After the events of June 1976, it had taken nine months for the fighting in South Africa to

The body of Richard Lebona, Jabulani, 17 August 1990.

subside. Five hundred men, women and children died. The current war looked set to kill the same number of people within three weeks.

I slept deeply at first, but woke around two. Judo lay on his back beside me, the two small blankets barely covering us. He had a monotonous, fluid cough. The cold air came in through the asbestos roof and seized hold of the blankets. I curled up on my side with one ear pressed into the mattress and the other covered by my right hand. But sleep and silence were both a long way off. Instead I seemed to hear the noise of the angry crowd outside Mapetla hostel; of Inkatha beating the vendors' sheds; of the grieving women following the body in the van. The last thing I heard was like a great scurrying of rats followed by the noise of angry school children marching out of the cemetery.

Photo: Ken Oosterbroek

Notes on Contributors

Simon Schama's 'Death of a Harvard Man' is an extract from his book *Dead Certainties (Unwarranted Speculations)*, which will be published by Granta Books next spring. It developed from his piece 'The Many Deaths of General Wolfe' which appeared in 'History', *Granta* 32. **William Boyd**'s novels include *An Ice-Cream War*, *A Good Man in Africa* and, most recently, *Brazzaville Beach*. **Jan Bogaerts** lives in the Netherlands; he is currently working on a photographic project on the Ivory Coast. **Geoffrey Wolff**'s book *The Final Club* was published in the summer. *The Duke of Deception: Memories of My Father* was recently re-issued by Vintage in Britain. He lives in Jamestown, Rhode Island. **Louise Erdrich**'s story 'Old Man Potchikoo' appeared in *Granta* 27. Her next book, *The Crown of Columbus*, jointly written with Michael Dorris, will be published in 1991. **Svetlana Alexiyevich** is the author of *War's Unwomanly Face*, a collection of Soviet women's memories of the Second World War. When 'Boys in Zinc' appeared in a Soviet journal the author received death threats and was forced into hiding. It is extracted from a book about the war in Afghanistan which has yet to be published in the Soviet Union. **Peregrine Hodson**'s last story for *Granta*, 'Thursday Night in Tokyo', appeared in *Granta* 28. He is currently working on a book, *A Circle Round the Sun*, which will be published by Heinemann next year. **Amitav Ghosh** is the author of *The Shadow Lines* and *The Circle of Reason*. His next book, about Egypt, will be published by Granta Books in the autumn of 1991. **Fouad Elkoury** lives in Paris. He was born in Beirut and is the author of a book of photographs of his home city, *Beyrouth—Aller-Retour*. **Don DeLillo**'s 'At Yankee Stadium' is taken from his novel *Mao II*, which will be published next summer by Jonathan Cape. Part one of 'Time's Arrow', **Martin Amis**'s work-in-progress, appeared in *Granta* 33. The third and final part will appear in the next issue. His last novel, *London Fields*, has just been published in paperback. **Jeremy Harding** is preparing a book on conflict in Africa, *Small Wars, Small Mercies*. His piece 'Polisario' appeared in *Granta* 26, 'Travel'.